Walking the Lir

CH00539466

Though there are some who will regard
most will take it more gently. If you wo
explore places of interest off the main 1
pace then you might make use of our div
sections, taking each section as a day
described both from south to north and 1
is optional. (Readers walking north to .
and use the book 'back to front'.)

Not everyone will fancy doing the whole Way at a stretch; in this case there
are two options; taking the more atractive parts as separate linear walks or
incorporating them into circular walks, so easing the transport problem.
Some suggestions for suitable rounds are made at the end of the book.

The authors gratefully acknowledge the
generous help of members of the Derbyshire
Dales group of the Ramblers Association and of
their Chairman Ken Hammond. Thanks also to
Phil Berry, Rights of Way Officer of the
Derbyshire Dales District Council for his
meticulous checking of the text.

The River Wye near Miller's Dale.

Walking the Limestone Way

together with the
Matlock Spur
Ashbourne Spur
& five circular walks

Ron & Elizabeth Haydock
Bill & Dorothy Allen

Scarthin Books
1997

THE COUNTRY CODE
Guard against all risk of fire
Fasten all gates
Keep dogs under proper control
Keep to paths across farmland
Avoid damaging fences, hedges and walls
Leave no litter
Safeguard water supplies
Protect wildlife, plants and trees
Go carefully on country roads
Respect the life of the countryside

Published by Scarthin Books, Cromford, Derbyshire, 1997
Phototypesetting by Techniset Typesetters, Newton-le-Willows
Printed by Redwood Books

Authors and publisher have taken pains to make this book accurate
and safe and can accept no responsibility for accidents and injuries
incurred whilst using it.

ISBN 0 907758 92 4

Contents

THE NEW LIMESTONE WAY
Rocester to Castleton

A walk from Matlock to Castleton was the full extent of the Limestone Way until in 1994 the District Councils of East Staffordshire, Staffordshire Moorlands, Derbyshire Dales and High Peak agreed to sponsor an extension south. As a result of the extension the length of the Way has increased from just over 40 kilometers to almost twice that distance. The shortest route no longer passes through Matlock but the missing section of the old walk has been included in this guide as a spur. A second spur, from Thorpe to Ashbourne, is also described, so there is the option of a walk from Ashbourne to Castleton.

The Way and the Matlock spur have been way-marked using yellow arrows on a brown disc (latterly green) and discs bearing the ram's head logo. Working parties from the Ramblers Association and Rotarians cooperated with footpaths officers of the District Councils to carry this out. The Ashbourne spur is not systematically way-marked but is entirely on public footpaths.

GUIDELINES

The Way takes you from the Midlands to the edge of the Pennine country, mainly along quiet paths through varied and often superb countryside. Because of the lead-mining in the past and quarrying for limestone and mining for fluorspar in the present some care is needed at times. Though most mine shafts along the route have been capped none of them should be assumed safe. Near disturbed ground stick closely to the Way and keep dogs under strict control. In the opinion of the District Councils the Way is unsuitable for mass sponsored walks. Heavy traffic may be expected on the occasional road section.

The route description is accompanied by strip maps so that no further aids to route-finding should be needed. Despite this we recommend the use of Ordnance Survey maps and a compass. Most of the Way is covered by the 1:25 000 Outdoor Leisure map number 24: *The Peak District – White Peak Area* and it is fully covered by 1:25 000 Pathfinder maps numbers 820 and 831. Use of maps and compass is advised for the circular walks.

In the matter of dress, no special gear is needed. Generally it will suffice to wear light windproof clothes and lightweight boots and carry a warmer garment and waterproofs. The going for most of the Way is over easy terrain but there are a few rocky places where you may be grateful for a bit of ankle support. In damp conditions limestone is 'greasy' and you will need good soles on your footwear.

FOLLOW THE COUNTRY CODE

In particular, please keep dogs under close control where there are farm animals. Bulls of certain breeds are permitted to graze in fields crossed by public footpaths; they will usually show no interest at all in you.

Transport and Accommodation

A linear walk always presents transport problems and as the Limestone Way passes through no large towns public transport services are sparse. Matlock (via Derby) and Hope (on the Manchester – Sheffield line) have railway stations. Matlock and Ashbourne are reached by short spurs from the main route and are good centres of accommodation. Hope is two miles east of Castleton. Information on trains may be obtained from any British Rail enquiry office, in particular those at Derby (Tel: 01332 257000) and Manchester (Tel: 0161 8328353).

Some towns and villages on the Way have regular bus services. **Peak District – Timetable** may be purchased from local Tourist Information offices or by post from

> Public Transport Unit
> Derbyshire County Council
> Chatsworth Hall
> Matlock
> Derbyshire DE4 3FW.

This publication gives full details of all trains and bus services in the Peak District as well as much other useful information. Details of buses serving Rocester are obtainable by ringing Stoke-on-Trent (01782) 747000. Brief details of services available:

Castleton 173 to Bakewell, 272 to Sheffield, 274 to Chesterfield
Miller's Dale 65 Sheffield – Buxton, 66 Chesterfield – Buxton
(A6 near) **Taddington** R1 Nottingham – Manchester, X23 Keele – Sheffield
Flagg 192 (circular, one direction only) to Buxton via Monyash
Monyash 192 circular route serving Flagg
Youlgreave 2 to Bakewell, 151 mini to Bakewell, 171 Middleton – Bakewell
Elton 170/172 Bakewell – Matlock, 170 Bakewell – Chesterfield
Winster as Elton
Upper Town 158 to Matlock via Bonsall
Swinscoe Hill 201 Derby – Manchester, via Ashbourne and Leek
Ellastone Uttoxeter – Belper via Ashbourne
Rocester 238,239 Cheadle – Uttoxeter. There is no Sunday service.

Other services on the Way run on certain dates only. To confirm information on buses in the Peak District you may call Busline on Buxton (01298) 23089. For walkers using their own transport car parks are marked on the strip maps, in information boxes or along the route.

Tourist Information Derbyshire Dales District Council operate tourist information centres in Ashbourne (Tel: 01335 343666) or Matlock Bath (Tel: 01629 55082). The Peak District National Park information office is in Bakewell (Tel: 01629 813227). East Staffordshire is covered from Burton upon Trent (Tel: 01283 616609) on Staffordshire Moorlands from Leek (Tel: 01538 381000). and High Peak from Buxton (Tel: 01298 25106).

The Peak District is a popular holiday area so it is advisable to book ahead; even a telephone call a few hours ahead of your arrival may serve to avoid an extra trudge at the end of a long day. On the other hand there is plenty of varied accommodation.

Hotels and Guest Houses

For full details ask for a copy of *Accommodation in the Derbyshire Dales*, revised annually and obtainable from the Tourist information offices in Ashbourne or Matlock Bath. The area covered includes Rocester but not Castleton. The Information Centre in Castleton (Tel: 01433 620679) publishes an annual *Accommodation and Catering* list covering the Peak National Park area.

Youth Hostels

There are hostels at Ilam Hall, 3 km from Thorpe (Tel: 01335 350212), Matlock (Tel: 01629 582983), Elton (Tel: 01629 650394), Youlgreave (Tel: 01629 636518), Ravenstor in Miller's Dale (Tel: 01298 871826) and Castleton (Tel: 01433 620235). For further information or a multiple booking you could contact the Central Region office (Tel: 01629 825850).

Camping

There are camp sites at Ashbourne (Sandybrook Hall, near Tissington Trail, open April to October, tel: 01335 342679), Grangemill (Middle Hills Farm, 2 km from Ible, open April to November, tel: 01629 582967), Birchover (Barn Farm, 2 km from the Way, open April to October, tel: 01629 650245), Youlgreave (Hopping Farm, 1 km from Way, open April to October, tel: 01629 636302), Monyash (Rawson House Farm, open April to November, tel: 01629 813521), Flagg (Street House Farm, Pomeroy, 2 kms from Way, open Easter to October, tel: 01298 83259), Castleton (Losehill Site, 1 km from end of walk, open end of May to October, tel: 01433 620636).

Camping without facilities may be possible on applying to farms along the way. In addition, for those who enjoy camping but would rather not tote a tent, there are camping barns providing shelter at low cost at Losehill Hall (2 km from Castleton, tel: 01433 620373), One Ash Grange (on Way, tel: 01629 636291), Middleton-by-Youlgreave (Castle Farm, 400 m from Way, tel: 01629 636746) and Taddington (1 km from Way, tel: 01298 85308 [day], 01298 85730 [evenings]). You can obtain a booklet about camping barns by calling 01433 620373.

Notes on the route descriptions

Distances have been given in kilometres (km) and metres (m) rather than miles and yards. We hope that the metric measures are now pretty familiar but, just in case, here are a few notes comparing them with the older alternatives.

A km is 1000 m which is about $\frac{5}{8}$ mile. To walk a km takes between 10 and 20 minutes (15 min. at $2\frac{1}{2}$ m.p.h.)

A metre is just over a yard. Add a tenth on to a distance in m to convert to an approximate distance in yards: 40 m is just under 44 yards, and so on.

Abbreviations and signs

BS – bus service   WC – public toilet   T – public telephone

CP – car park   PH – public house   /F – serving food   C – café

■ – building   Sh – shop   PO – post office   ⬛ – church

g – gate   s – stile   fb – footbridge   fp – footpath

– woodland   – river or stream

– Limestone Way   – other footpaths (where shown)

– farm track or drive   – metalled road

– stone wall (where shown)   – field boundary (where shown)

GR – Ordnance Survey grid reference

ETL – (overhead) electricity transmission lines

N, S, E, W – North, South, East, West   L, R – left, right

→ – continue in the same direction

Generally, a **road** has a good metalled surface,
       a **drive** is the approach to a farmhouse intended for cars,
       a **track** is rougher but may be used by tractors.

A direction given, say, as N is only approximately North. More accurate compass bearings are given in degrees in a few places. Tricky or dangerous parts of the route are indicated by **bold print**, alternative footpaths by *italics*.

The Limestone Way has been abbreviated simply to 'The Way' throughout; no mystical connotation is intended!

9

Limestone Way Country — an introduction

Geology and Topography

The Limestone Way runs from Rocester in N. E. Staffordshire to Castleton in N. Derbyshire. From Rocester to Mayfield the underlying rocks are Triassic sandstone, the hills smooth and the soil reddish in colour, but near Thorpe the landscape changes, the terrain becoming more deeply rugged with outcrops of grey limestone. A central plateau of carboniferous limestone, roughly 10 miles wide, stretches from Castleton in the north almost to Ashbourne in the south, and is bordered on north, east and west by an uneven band of millstone grit.

The principal rivers, the Dove and the Derwent, flow from north to south towards the River Trent, and they and their tributaries have cut deeply into the soft, soluble limestone to produce the steep-sided dales so characteristic of the area.

The geology has had a profound effect on the industrial development of the Peak District. In the past the lead deposits that occurred in the limestone were very important. North of Ballidon, where positive evidence of Roman lead-mining activity has been found at Royston Grange Farm, the Way passes through an area that is believed to have been producing lead since Roman and Saxon times. Seven lead mines are recorded in the Matlock and Bakewell areas in Domesday Book. By the 17th Century lead was mined extensively in this part of Derbyshire and for a time Winster was the centre of the most important lead producing area in Britain. Today limestone is quarried for roadstone and agricultural use.

Early Roads and Transport

The earliest routes date from neolithic and Bronze Age times and linked the henge monuments, e.g. Arbor Low and the Nine Stone Circle on Harthill Moor, and iron age forts and burial grounds (tumuli). Later major routes probably derived from the Saxon port-weg, literally a route to a market town. The medieval portways were very important trade routes carrying lead and other minerals out of the area and bringing salt, textiles and other essential goods on the return journey.

Traces of Roman roads are also found in The Street, a direct route between Derby and Buxton, Batham Gate from Buxton to Navio, a Roman fort near Brough, and Hereward Street, which ran from Rocester through Ellastone and Mayfield, forded the Derwent at Cromford, and continued towards Chesterfield and Sheffield.

Local placenames often provide evidence of old roads and former mining grounds. From medieval times an intricate network of packhorse ways developed. The packhorse's loads were carried in panniers and the trains were in the charge of a 'jagger'. Some stretches of the routes were roughly paved, while others were 'holloways' in fields and hillsides. In places the

Limestone Way follows these ancient tracks and the paths used by the lead miners to reach their mining grounds.

Settlements

Rocester, Buxton, Brough and Chesterfield are known to have been Roman settlements. Many of the central villages grew up near the lead mines and show a similar development pattern. Hamlets expanded as lead mining grew in importance, followed by a period of rapid development and relative prosperity during the 17th century and then a general decline as the veins were worked out and cheaper lead became available elsewhere. There was some alternative employment available in the quarries and in agriculture but it was not until improved transport and services made the villages attractive to commuters that there was much further development and revitalisation. Today the lovely villages in beautiful countryside attract residents, but unfortunately high property prices and restricted local facilities lead to younger families moving to nearby towns.

Lead Mining

Anyone could register a claim to a lead vein, except under a highway, or within a churchyard, orchard or private garden, and the claimants were given the right to use available water to wash the ore, and had the right of passage to and from their plots. Many of the field paths, often marked by a series of squeezers, were originally miner's tracks.

Lead was transported by packhorse at first and later by horse-drawn carts. Miners frequently worked their meers independently combining working a smallholding with mining. Small fields, many with a stone barn, are found near some mining grounds, and good examples can be seen near Winster. By the 17th century lead mining was of great importance in north Derbyshire with increasing use of machinery to bring the ore to the surface and to drain the levels. Underground drains, locally known as 'soughs' were also constructed. Smelting was originally done on small hearths, the blast provided by hand bellows, but wind-powered smelters were built on high hills known as 'bole-hills; while later still blast-hearth furnaces were built, and narrow rail systems used to move the raw and finished materials.

Several of the mining villages, particularly Brassington, Winster and Bonsall, expanded rapidly and the mining industry provided employment for many people in addition to the miners themselves. By 1880 leadmining had almost died out in Derbyshire and the villages declined with it. Fluorspar, a by-product of lead mining, was originally largely ignored but early in the 20th century it was realised that quantities remained in the 'hillocks' or spoil heaps around the mines. It is now extracted from old waste heaps, refined by a flotation process and used in the manufacture of non-stick pans, aerosol propellants and toothpastes. Today quarrying for limestone is an important local industry, barytes is extracted for use in the paper and paint industries while calcite is mined for gravel for paths and for terrazzo work.

Natural History

The Limestone Way passes through a richly varied landscape and enthusiastic geologists and naturalists will find much to interest them.

Fossils and minerals may be found in the abandoned limestone quarries and mine spoil heaps.

Some of the river valleys in limestone country are dry, or dry in summer, because the river waters seep through the porous underlying rocks, or are diverted into soughs, to follow an underground course and emerge further downstream or perhaps from caves. Water fowl and river birds are found near the rivers and skylarks and linnets can be heard above the fields. Lapwings are still fairly common. Hovering kestrels and sparrowhawks hunt from the air while magpies and jays seek their prey in the fields and hedges. Smaller birds such as dunnocks, wrens, goldcrests and redstarts nest in hedges and shrubs.

Rabbits are common all through the year but hares are mainly sighted in spring time. Although there are many foxes and badgers they are wary and not often seen.

A thousand varieties of flowering plants have been identified in Derbyshire, some of them peculiar to limestone country. The spring and summer are a particular delight. Wood anemones and wood sorrel, and later bluebells, carpet the woodlands, primroses appear on the banks of streams and lanes, and cowslips and buttercups in the fields. Germander speedwell and tormentil are followed by cranesbill, red campion, herb robert, foxgloves and cow parsley. Ramsons, or wild garlic has a very distinctive smell when trodden on, and Sweet Cecily, which has an aniseed scent, can sometimes be found.

Rarer plants of the area include Jacob's ladder (there is a colony in Lathkill Dale) and orchids which are sometimes found near abandoned lead mines. The spoil heaps support yellow pansies, milkworts, vetches and rock roses.

In summer there are many butterflies, among them the lovely common blue which is the exact colour of the harebells it visits. The brimstone, orange tip, dark green fritillary and small heath butterflies can be easily identified.

The fragmentary woodland is mainly remnants of ancient deciduous forest. Sessile oak and ash predominate and silver birch and rowan add colour in spring and autumn. Hawthorn, known locally as May blossom, brightens the hedges in May and June and its bright red berries decorate them in the autumn.

Rocester to Thorpe

Although it is now a small township with fewer than 2000 inhabitants Rocester has been continuously occupied since about 600 BC. Celtic tribes originally dominated the area but about 48 AD the Romans established Rowcestre as a permanent fort to house 500 or 1000 troops to control the area and guard the important road system, particularly the route from Derby towards Stoke. There are traces of the fort in a field north of the church.

The Limestone Way starts at the south end of West View, near the old Tutbury Mill. This was originally a corn mill but in the 18th century Richard Arkwright, the inventor of the spinning frame and a pioneer of water-powered machinery, had it converted to process cotton. The Abbey Field, to the west of West View, contains mounds indicating the original site of the buildings of St. Mary's Augustinian Priory which was founded in 1441. The monks were unpopular locally because of dubious financial dealings and poor morals and the order was disbanded in 1538. Although a manor house, Rocester Hall, was later built on the site this too was derelict by the mid-1600s.

Today Rocester is dominated by the factory of J. C. Bamford Excavators Ltd on the outskirts of the town. This highly successful company has given much support to archaeological excavations locally, particularly during 1985–1987. At the back of St. Michael's Church there is an interesting photographic record of the digs and a small display of artefacts found, together with a brief description, with maps, of Rocester's development. In the churchyard there is a well-preserved 13th century cross and against the wall between the lych-gate and the church door are old gravestones with some interesting epitaphs.

The Way proceeds towards Barrowhill Farm where there is a small hill fort, evidence of pre-Roman settlement, and then downhill to the River Dove and past Doveleys, formerly a school, to Ellastone Bridge.

Ellastone is a straggling village with some fine old houses and is the 'Hayslope' of George Eliot's novel 'Adam Bede'. Her father, Robert Evans, spent his early life here and his father is buried in the churchyard. Robert Evans was the model for Adam Bede, and Seth Bede was based on his brother Samuel. Beyond the church, in Upper Ellastone, is Adam Bede's cottage.

The church contains memorials to the residents of Calwich Abbey which was originally founded in Norman times. The monks were driven out in 1530 and the buildings bought by John Fleetwood who converted it into a home. His descendents built Wootton Lodge a few miles away and the Abbey was sold to Bernard Granville and later rebuilt. Granville had many famous friends who are recorded as visiting Calwich, among them Handel, who gave Granville a manuscript copy of his works, and is reputed to have composed his Water Music in a small pavilion in the Abbey grounds, Rousseau (in 1776) and also Anna Seward, the 'Swan of Lichfield'.

The Way continues west of Mayfield towards Blore, where Buckingham's Field recalls the incident when the Cavalier George Villiers, second Duke of Buckingham, fleeing after the battle of Worcester in 1651 at the end of the Civil War, was sheltered and hidden in a cottage after he fell from his horse and broke his arm.

Shortly after Blore the Way crosses the River Dove, the boundary between Staffordshire and Derbyshire, at Coldwall Bridge, and then rises towards Thorpe Green.

Thorpe's very attractive church, with its fine Norman tower, is usually open ('Walkers welcome but please check your boots before entering'), and dates from about 1100. The church has a tub font, one of three in Derbyshire, which is believed to date from the 11th century. Originally it was carved but neglect and 'restoration' in the early 19th century destroyed much of the decoration. A similar unrestored font can be seen at Tissington a little further along the Way.

The outer doorway in the south porch of St Leonard's church has marks said to have been caused by arrow sharpening. In the 14th century after the Black Death, which seriously reduced the number of available archers, a general decree ordered Sunday afternoons to be devoted to archery practice 'on the south side of the church' and stores of bows and arrows were often maintained in parish churches for the use of those unable to afford their own.

Not all walls are so high . . .

15

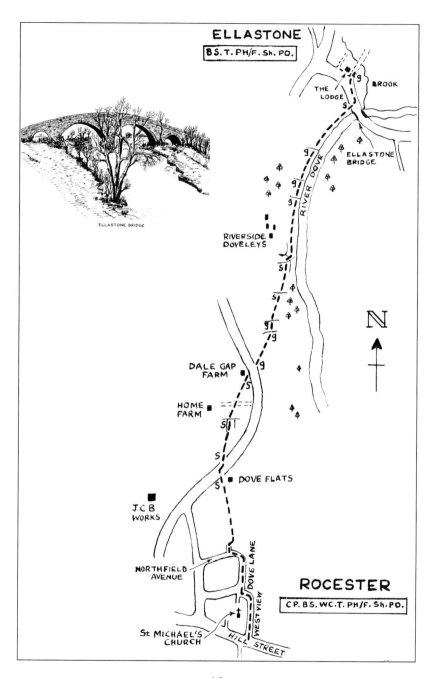

ELLASTONE

B.S.T. PH/F. Sh. PO.

THE LODGE

BROOK

ELLASTONE BRIDGE

RIVER DOVE

RIVERSIDE DOVELEYS

ELLASTONE BRIDGE

N

DALE GAP FARM

HOME FARM

DOVE FLATS

JCB WORKS

NORTHFIELD AVENUE

St MICHAEL'S CHURCH

DOVE LANE

WEST VIEW

HILL STREET

ROCESTER

CP. BS, WC.T. PH/F. Sh. PO.

Rocester — Calwich Abbey Lodge

 South — North   North — South

From Hill Street (on Staffordshire Way) walk via West View around churchyard into Dove Lane. Turn R along Dove Lane.

Where Northfield Avenue starts turn R up track, cross bridge and follow hedge uphill → to B5030. Turn R up B5030 for 50 m.

Take stile on L and follow fence uphill in hollow way. After stile bear slightly R towards oak tree on near sky-line.

Cross drive → to top corner of field. Take stile on to B5030 by Dalesgap Farm.

Cross directly over road → through three metal gates, over a stile and pass a stand of scotch pines.

After a further stile turn R down a steep bank to River Dove.

Follow river upstream for a km, through kissing gates. As you pass a small wood you see Ellastone ahead.

Climb stile by Ellastone Bridge and turn L along road. In 100 m you reach lodge to Calwich Abbey.

At lodge turn L along road to Ellastone Bridge, then follow River Dove downstream for a km, through kissing-gates.

Bear R steeply up a bank then take a line a little W of S towards a stand of scotch pines.

→ over a stile and through three metal gates to road at Dalegap Farm.

Cross B5030, take stile, → towards oak. →, cross drive → to stile in corner of field. Follow fence down to B5030. Turn R down B5030 for 50 m.

Take stile on L and follow hedge → to bridge ditch and reach houses of Rocester, → to Northfield Avenue. Bear L into Dove Lane.

At end of lane turn L into ginnel and around churchyard into West View. → to end of way in Hill Road (on Staffordshire Way).

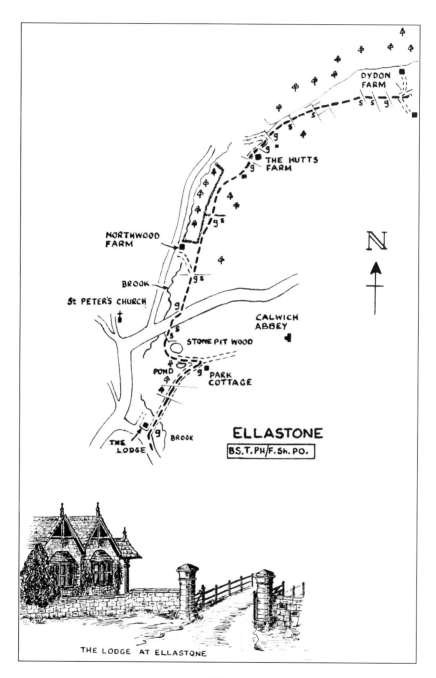

DYDON FARM

THE HUTTS FARM

NORTHWOOD FARM

BROOK

St PETER'S CHURCH

CALWICH ABBEY

STONE PIT WOOD

POND

PARK COTTAGE

THE LODGE

BROOK

N

ELLASTONE

BS.T.PH/F.Sh.PO.

THE LODGE AT ELLASTONE

Calwich Abbey Lodge — Dydon Farm

↑ South — North
North — South

Turn R along drive, through fine oak gate, to brick-built Park Cottage on R. On L, among trees, is Martin's Pond.

Pass through a gateway then **sharp** L along a grassy track. A little later you see Ellastone Church. Way here bears gradually R around mound of Stonepit Wood.

Leave broad track and bear half R to a stile in a double fence. → to stile taking you to B5032.

Turn R up B5032 for 130 m and through a gateway on L. Head slightly E of N (bearing 15° magnetic), through a metal gateway and over a stile.

Ignore track on L and walk parallel to brook, then to R of wall above woodland.

Bear slightly R to a stile by a metal gate, then towards a corrugated metal shed on skyline. Cross field to shed and → by metal gates to drive of Hutts Farm.

Take farm drive to metal gate on R. Turn R through gate and follow fence along green track. → through two stiles.

→, aiming to L of hedge end on skyline. →, contouring to apparent large tree (twin sycamores).

→ with hedge on R to stile in corner of field. Turn slightly R and ascend to gate.

→ with hedge on L and cross farm drive (of Dydon Farm) by oak tree.

Cross farm track by oak tree and → with hedge on R to metal gate. Go through gate and turn slightly R to stile.

Contour with hedge and later stone wall on L. When wall ends → towards end of hedge-line.

→ to green track with woodland beyond fence on R. → to farm drive. Turn L to Hutts Farm.

Take drive between buildings, through two gateways. In field ahead pass to R of corrugated iron building and cross field, using tip of a patch of woodland as a direction marker.

In corner of field climb stile by metal gate. Bear slightly L alongside wall. Wall turns sharp R but → parallel to brook. Note Ellastone Church on R.

Climb a stile, → to a metal gate and reach B5032. Turn R for 130 m down road.

Just before Ellastone name-sign take stile on L and make for stile in double fence, cutting corner of field.

Join a grassy track bearing L around mound of Stonepit Wood. Through a metal gate enter a short stretch of grassy track. Martin's Pond is among trees on R.

Go through gateway with concrete posts then **sharp** R to join main drive from Calwich Abbey. Follow drive to road.

19

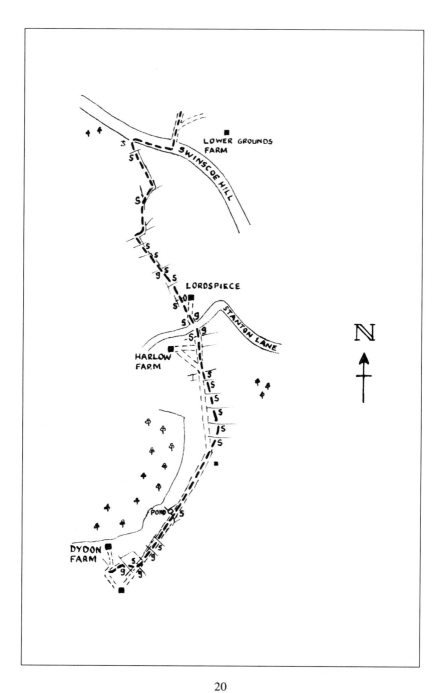

LOWER GROUNDS FARM

SWINSCOE HILL

LORDSPIECE

STANTON LANE

HARLOW FARM

POND

DYDON FARM

N

Dydon Farm — Swinscoe Hill

 South — North   **North — South**

→. Turn half R at metal gate then half L at stile, to follow hedge. → through gateways and stiles. Where small pond appears on L follow track.

After 400 m take ladder stile on R and → along ridge. Middle Mayfield lies to R.

Having passed a holly hedge on R turn slightly L, with a hedge on L. 100 m on a concealed stile returns you to track.

Follow track to Stanton Lane and cross to entrance to Lordspiece Farm. Follow hedge on L ahead and over stile by small pond.

→. After next stile bear slightly R. →, keeping hedge on R, then heading towards farm at top of hill.

→ with hedge on R. When hedge turns sharp R continue to follow it to stile.

→, hedge on R. At next corner turn L and up field to a stile. → to A52 via waste ground (result of road-straightening).

After stile, Way turns sharply to L, almost back on itself. Diverge gradually from road to next stile.

→. At end of field do **not** take stile ahead but turn R around field to stile.

→ along boundary of next field then bear L, following hedge on L. Continue to follow hedge when it turns sharply to L.

Next stile is not by gate but slightly to R. → through four stiles, pass a small pond on L and follow fence on R to entrance to Lordspiece Farm.

Cross Stanton Lane and take track between hedges. After 200 m take stile on L. → with hedge on R.

After next stile turn slightly L. Cross two fields keeping hedge on R. At next stile turn slightly R, with holly hedge on L.

→ along ridge with Middle Mayfield on L. → to rejoin track by ladder stile. →, following track for 400 m.

Pass small pond on R and climb stile by gate. Follow hedge on L. Do not go through gateway towards farm but between hedges.

→ with hedge on R. On reaching stile on R make half-turn to R to gateway, then half-turn L, following hedge on R, then crossing farm drive by oak tree.

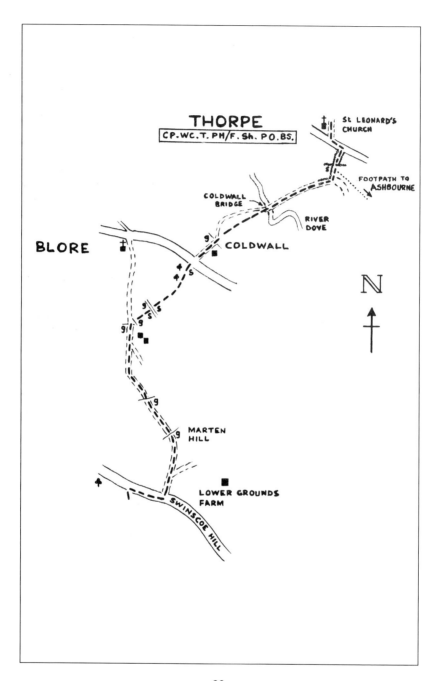

THORPE
CP.WC.T.PH/F.Sh.PO.BS.

St LEONARD'S
CHURCH

FOOTPATH TO
ASHBOURNE

COLDWALL
BRIDGE

RIVER
DOVE

BLORE

COLDWALL

N

MARTEN
HILL

LOWER GROUNDS
FARM

SWINSCOE HILL

Swinscoe Hill — Thorpe

↑ South — North   **North — South ↓**

Cross A52, turn R and walk down verge for 250 m. Turn L to take a metalled drive. After 50 m go through a gate.

After a further 50 m keep L at a fork then continue on road for 1200 m to Woodhouses, on R.

→ through two gates and in 20 m find gate on R into a field. Bear, passing under ETL at right angles.

→ downhill, fence and hedge on R. At bottom, cross ditch to metal gate and → for 400 m, later following line of oak trees.

Cross road and take drive → past Coldwall Farm → through gate and downhill. In a short while you see Coldwall Bridge over River Dove.

Cross bridge, ignore track on R and follow farm road uphill for almost a km, enjoying fine views down Dove valley.

On reaching signpost just before brow of hill follow wall as it bends L steeply uphill. Continue along wallside through stile.

→ along track to road. Bear L along road for 20 m. Take track (Church Lane) on R, past brick-built cottage. Descend for 300 m. At bottom bear L across grassy wasteland to road at Thorpe Green.

At Thorpe Green, opposite St Leonard's Cottage, turn L with fence on L across grassy wasteland.

After 100 m turn R up track (Church Lane). In 150 m you pass stile leading to Ashbourne spur, on L. → a further 150 m to road. Turn L along road for 20 m then R along a grassy track.

→ through stile, along walled track, then bear R steeply downhill to farm road. Turn R down road for a km, enjoying fine views S across valley of River Dove.

As you approach Coldwall Bridge Coldwall Farm may be seen ahead on horizon. Cross bridge and bear slightly L uphill towards farm.

Take metal gate on to track past farm and on to road. Cross directly and → following line of oak trees. Woodhouses may be seen on hillside ahead.

→ to metal gate in corner of field. →, crossing ditch, towards Woodhouses.

Approaching farm bear slightly L, passing under ETL at right angles to gate in corner of field.

Turn L along road, through gates, past Woodhouses and a further 1300 m to A52.

Turn R, keeping on verge and walk up A52 for 250 m. Cross road and waste ground (result of road-straightening) to find stile.

Thorpe to Ible

Pleasant paths from Thorpe, a short stretch of road leading to an impressive gateway and a recently replanted avenue of lime trees, are a fitting entry to Tissington, one of Derbyshire's loveliest villages and well worth exploring. Tissington Hall, home of the Fitzherbert family for over 400 years, occupies most of the western side of a broad main street with the church, pond, old village school and some most attractive cottages grouped at the south end and the post office, a shop and more dwellings at the north end.

St Mary's Church was built soon after 1100 and has several original Norman features including a doorway with an attractive carved tympanum, and a tub-shaped font with symbolic carvings. As with Thorpe Church the porch shows evidence of arrow sharpening. The pulpit is a modified 'double-decker' and the unusual Fitzherbert memorial dates back to 1619.

Tissington is believed to be the first Derbyshire village to have introduced well dressing. During a long period of drought in the 17th century the springs continued to flow and in thanksgiving the wells were decorated with flowers. This became an annual festival and each year, at Ascensiontide, the five wells are decorated with elaborate and beautiful pictures made of flower petals, seeds, foliage and other materials pressed into a foundation of clay within a wooden frame. The wells are blessed during a traditional service and the well-dressings are left in place for about a week so that they can be visited and admired. Bonsall and Youlgreave, also on the Way, have well-dressing weeks.

The Way passes through the churchyard and into farmland. A bridge goes over the Tissington Trail, a walking and cycling route between Ashbourne and Hartington, which has been developed on a disused railway route. At Hartington it joins the High Peak Trail, a similar route which runs from Cromford almost to Buxton. A pleasant walk through typical limestone country leads to Parwich, a quiet village of grey stone houses grouped round the church and village greens. The church is of Norman origin, and contains a Norman font, but has been much restored.

The small village of Ballidon is a dusty place, dominated by the giant Tilcon quarries which are hidden behind a limestone hill to the north of the farms and cottages. A pretty church, with a small bell tower, stands in a walled enclosure, isolated from the other buildings. The church is usually locked but is reputed to show evidence of Norman origins and, together with Tissington church, once belonged to the monks of Dunstable. The Way passes near the church and then over the hill where it joins a grassy track, perhaps the original route from Ballidon to Brassington, and crosses the Ashbourne – Bakewell road on a rather dangerous corner. A short stretch of road leads to hummocky land, typical of abandoned lead mining grounds, from which there are fine views of Carsington Reservoir to the southeast with the roofs of Brassington village in the foreground. Brassington is another attractive village and accommodation and supplies can be obtained there.

A kilometre after crossing the High Peak Trail the Way reaches a section of the Portway by which it proceeds to Grangemill, where it crosses the Via Gellia, the main road between Cromford and Newhaven. A field path which climbs to skirt a quarry starts near the Holly Bush public house and leads to Ible, a remote village of farms and cottages. At the road side in the centre of the village there is an unusual series of spring-fed troughs, which once provided the main water supply for the village and water for horses and cattle. There is a post box on a farm wall, two signs offering bed and breakfast, and the Methodist chapel has been converted to a cottage, but Ible seems a village from a past era. D. H. Lawrence, who lived at nearby Middleton for a short time in 1908, knew it, and his short story 'Wintry Peacock' is set in (T)Ible. The long narrow fields probably developed from the open-field system of the Middle Ages. The original strips allocated were later exchanged and joined together to make small elongated fields which could be more easily cultivated, and then enclosed by stone walls to keep cattle in (or out!)

IN MEMORY OF JOSEPH HODGKINSON 1927
TISSINGTON CHURCHYARD

25

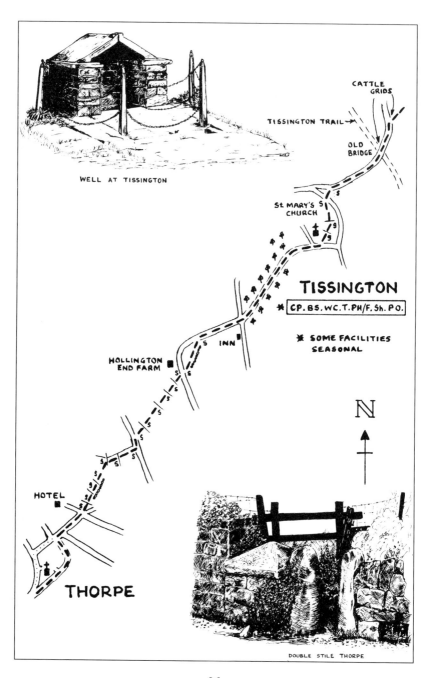

WELL AT TISSINGTON

CATTLE GRIDS

TISSINGTON TRAIL →

OLD BRIDGE

St MARY'S CHURCH

TISSINGTON

CP. BS. WC. T. PH/F. Sh. PO.

✳ SOME FACILITIES SEASONAL

HOLLINGTON END FARM

INN

N

HOTEL

THORPE

DOUBLE STILE THORPE

Thorpe — Tissington Trail

 South — North   **North — South**

At Thorpe Green turn R along road for 300 m to Peveril of Peak Hotel. Cross road and stile by name-sign of hotel, then another stile. **Make for tree by wall ahead.** → to enter National Trust ground and turn R along wallside.

Keep by wall, passing sheepfold, going through gate and over stile. Walk uphill, ditch on R, to stile in corner of field. → over two stiles to Spend Lane. Turn L up lane for 60 m. Leave lane, making a half-turn R, then → by stiles to stile near entrance to Hollington End Farm.

Cross road, take stile and proceed with wall on R to Washbrook Lane. Turn R up lane to A515. Cross road and → along drive for 800 m to St Mary's Church, Tissington. Enter churchyard.

A few m along drive climb flight of seven steps on R and follow wall on R to wooden gate near corner. → through gateway by drinking trough. Make a half-turn L and follow wall on L. → across Chapel Lane through a further two stiles to another lane.

Turn R along lane for 500 m to bridge Tissington Trail. At sign of Shaw's Farm there is an extensive view ahead of typical limestone country. Take track towards Shaw's Farm.

Bridge Tissington Trail and continue along lane for 500 m. Turn L through a stile, cross field and take a further stile into Chapel Lane. Cross directly and follow hedge line on R down field.

Go through gateway by drinking trough. Turn half-R to find in far corner stile and wooden gate into St Mary's churchyard. → alongside wall, passing village hall on L to take flight of steps to church drive.

Leave churchyard, cross village green and take road signed Dovedale. In 800 m reach and cross A515 to take road to Thorpe. After 300 m, at bottom of hill go through stile on L.

Take route with stream on L, then follow field boundary, bearing slightly R. Cross road to stile near entrance to Hollington End Farm. Stiles may be seen in line ahead.

Follow stiles to Spend Lane, noting Thorpe Cloud away to R. Go down lane for 60 m then turn R through stile and proceed with wall on R. After another stile on R follow ditch downfield.

In corner of field stile takes you by side of sheepfold. → to leave National Trust land and →, cutting off corner of field, to stile, noting Peveril of Peak hotel on R. Bear slightly L to stiles to road.

Cross road to take pavement into Thorpe. On reaching Thorpe Cottage on L, at Thorpe Green, road bends R but Way goes down rough grassland to L, alongside garden fence.

BALLIDON CHURCH

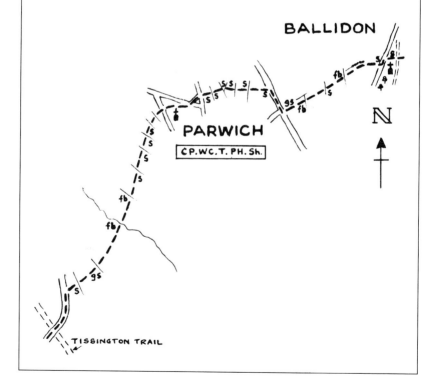

BALLIDON

PARWICH

CP.WC.T. PH. Sh.

N

TISSINGTON TRAIL

Tissington Trail — Ballidon Church

 South — North   **North — South**

After 100 m down track turn R directly downhill to stile. → through stile/gate and continue downhill with hedge on R. Diverge slightly to L over fb.

→, making for ETL pole. At top of hill bridge ditch and bear slightly L, following hedge on L. After a further stile Parwich is seen ahead. Way will pass its church, St Peter's.

→ through stile. Near end of hedge line find stile in wall on L. Follow wall on R and →, finally between house fence and wall, to join drive, bending R towards church.

On reaching road turn L along it for 40 m, then R, passing church on R. At playground sign turn L along minor road and follow wall on R. Take stile and go alongside house.

Bear slightly L to stile and → to further stile. Turn R and follow fence and hedge on R to stile at top of hill. →, hedge on R, to road. Turn R along road for 220 m.

At road junction turn L through stile signed Ballidon and proceed parallel to hedge line on L. **Watch carefully for concrete fb over ditch on L.** Cross fb and cut off corner of field to stile. Bear slightly L towards R end of line of trees ahead.

After a further stile and fb walk parallel to hedge on L to road. Turn L along road for 25 m, then R to church through stile. Pass church on your R, noting village on L and →, walking directly across track.

Pass church on your L and reach road via stile. Turn L along road for 25 m and take stile on R. follow sign to Parwich, with wall, later hedge, on R. Bridge ditch and bear slightly L to stile. → to further stile and then bridge over ditch in corner of field.

Walk with hedge on R, diverging slightly L towards end of field to stile onto road. Turn R up road for 220 m, turning off by stile to L just before brow of hill.

Follow hedge line on L towards Parwich ahead. After a stone squeeze stile turn L, then → towards houses. Walk between houses and via stile to road. Continue towards St Peter's Church.

Pass church on your L and continue to T-junction. Turn L along road towards Ashbourne. After 40 m turn sharp R along drive leading to garage. Here turn R to find stile.

Follow fp between houses. On reaching field bear slightly L (bearing 197° magnetic) to stile. Follow hedge line on R to bridge ditch. Shaw's Farm may be seen ahead. → downhill to wooden fb over stream.

→ towards hedge line on L. Take stile/gate and → uphill with field boundary on L to reach farm drive. Turn L up drive to fine bridge over Tissington Trail.

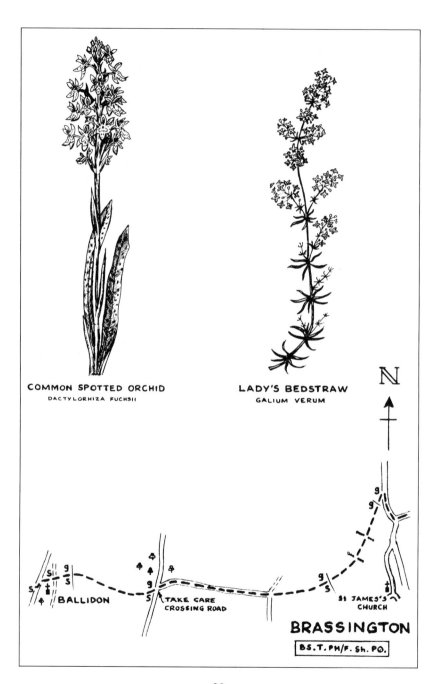

COMMON SPOTTED ORCHID
DACTYLORHIZA FUCHSII

LADY'S BEDSTRAW
GALIUM VERUM

N

BALLIDON

TAKE CARE
CROSSING ROAD

St JAMES'S
CHURCH

BRASSINGTON

BS.T. PH/F. Sh. PO.

Ballidon Church — Brassington

↑ South — North   **North — South ↓**

→ to top of hill and stile by metal gate. →
towards wall bending to L, on L. Join grassy
track and follow it to road, in deep dale. Cross
road and take Pasture Lane, passing ruins on
L.

Follow lane for 1 km. When it turns sharp R
carry straight on, following fp sign, up Lots
Lane, a grassy track, for 450 m.

When lane bends R past metal gate take stile
on L by wooden gate →: **do not follow clear
track at right angles to lane.**

**Route-finding is tricky over the next
section, of rough, disturbed ground.** Walk
with ETL on your L to find opening in wall
ahead. → on a magnetic bearing of 45°.

Go through gateway, then → through
gateways to Longcliffe-Brassington road.
Turn R and follow road downhill towards
Brassington for 230 m.

On reaching T-junction turn R up road
towards Longcliffe for 230 m and take metal
gate on L. **The next section is over rough,
disturbed ground. Route-finding is difficult
and stiles obscure.** Turn sharp L through the
gateway, making for a point slightly L of
highest part of field (bearing 225° magnetic).

Pass through a stone gateway and continue in
approximately same direction (bearing 220°
magnetic). A wall is reached near an ETL. →
roughly parallel to ETL. Go through gap in
wall and bear slightly R, passing beneath ETL
to stile by wooden gate.

Turn R down farm track (Lots Lane) for
450 m to join metalled Pasture Lane. → down
lane for 1 km to reach B5056 Ballidon-
Longcliffe Road. Cross over, slightly L, to
stile.

Take clearly defined grassy track to wind up
out of steep-sided dale. Approaching a
wooden gate Way turns slightly to L away
from track above a line of hawthorn trees to
stile in wall ahead, by a metal gate.

→ towards All Saints, small parish church of
Ballidon, crossing directly over a track just
before church.

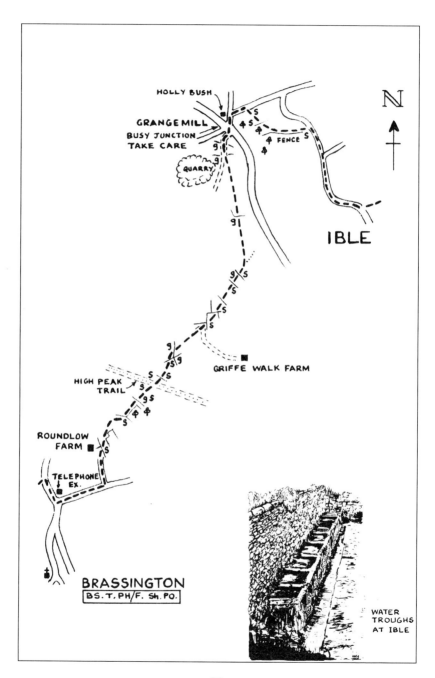

HOLLY BUSH

GRANGE MILL
BUSY JUNCTION
TAKE CARE

QUARRY

FENCE

IBLE

GRIFFE WALK FARM

HIGH PEAK
TRAIL

ROUNDLOW
FARM

TELEPHONE
EX.

BRASSINGTON
BS.T.PH/F. Sh.PO.

N

WATER
TROUGHS
AT IBLE

Brassington — Ible

 South — North   **North — South**

As road bends R turn L up minor road by telephone exchange (direction Wirksworth, Cromford). After 300 m take track on L to Roundlow Farm. On reaching corrugated iron shed turn L and through a stile to take clearly defined track ahead.

When track peters out → towards corner of wall. → to stile on L just before metal gate. Continue down field, stone wall on R, to squeeze stile, one of whose uprights is a London and NW railway boundary post.

Cross High Peak trail directly and →, over stiles. Make for farm track ahead and take it to corner of field, then leave it to take stile ahead. Bear slightly L, then Way takes you over four large fields, bearing gradually to R after first stile.

Take stile by gates and signpost, following bridleway to Grangemill, heading towards electricity pylon. → through a gateway and →, contouring to pass through another gateway and reach a track.

Follow track through gateway to A5012. Cross directly and take Bakewell Road for 40 m, then turn R along minor road for 55 m.

Climb bank and take stile on R, following direction indicated by signpost and later following wall on L, then fence on R.

At top of fence take stile onto road and turn R to follow road for 750 m through village of Ible.

After 750 m, having passed through village of Ible, road bends to L and starts to descend. Take stile on L and walk downhill with fence on L. When fence bends L bear slightly to R through broken wall and descend obliquely by stiles to minor road.

Turn L along road and L again at next T-junction to reach A5012 by Holly Bush Inn. Cross directly over A5012 and take track through gateway.

After 140 m bear slightly L, contouring hillside towards electricity pylon. go through gateways and → climbing steadily to top corner of large field. Take stile by gates and bear slightly R, following sign to Brassington.

→ over two large fields then bear slightly L to cross a third. → to a stile leading to a field with a farm track. Follow field boundary on R to join track. In far corner take stile by second metal gate.

Now head towards L of group of trees at top of field and take stiles to walk directly across High Peak Trail, following sign to Brassington. (One of uprights of squeeze stile is an old London and NW railway boundary post.)

Walk uphill, wall on L, then take stile by gateway. → with wall on L and go through stile. Bear R, wall on R, then slightly to L and → to farm track. Follow track past wall of bungalow.

When track reaches road turn R along it. In 300 m at T-junction turn R up road towards Longcliffe for 230 m.

The curious wood and lead seat on the Way near Winster.

Ible to Youlgreave

Beyond Ible the Way follows old miners' paths, marked by a series of squeezers, to the Bonsall lead mines. There is evidence of long abandoned opencast mines in two parallel hollows, one near the Way being quite deep, and grass-covered waste hillocks, while the footpaths to Slaley, Bonsall Dale and Uppertown indicate where miners lived and ore was taken for smelting.

The way ascends past farms and cottages to Upper Town where there is an attractive well-head in the high wall. From Hollins Farm the path to Moorlands Lane is marked by squeezers.

From Luntor Rocks, reputed to have been the scene of a murder, there is another old right of way which crosses the main road near a Lead Ore House, the best preserved example in the Peak district. Ore was tipped down a chute at the back into the ore house and securely stored until sold to the smelters in Winster.

Winster is a very attractive village and worth a detour. The main street is lined with fine houses, many dating from the heyday of lead mining. The Market House was built in the 16th century and was bought by the National Trust in 1906. It now houses a small N. T. information room. Although mentioned in the Domesday book, Winster's main development dates from the lead mining boom in the 1600s. By the 18th century it was well-known for its market, when rows of stalls lined the main road, but there is none held today. A pancake race still takes place each Shrove Tuesday.

There was once a small hamlet, Islington, near the Miner's Standard pub. The dwellings have gone but the small fields on each side of Islington Lane, many with a typical stone barn, still support a wide variety of crops and livestock. Mosey Mere, a reedy pond almost opposite the Lead Ore House, owes its continuing existence to an underlying layer of volcanic rock, and once provided the water supply for Islington.

Sweet Cecily, which has a strong aniseed smell, is abundant in the verges of Islington Lane which with Dudwood Lane and the paved track which leads up to Robin Hood's Stride are part of the old Portway.

Robin Hood's Stride, also known as Mock Beggar's Hall or Castle, is the subject of several legends. Its two pillars are called Weasel Pinnacle and Inaccessible Pinnacle and are 20 metres apart. One legend suggest that Robin Hood and Little John fired their arrows at the pillars from rocks some $2\frac{1}{2}$ kilometres away. Little John's arrow hit the rocks but Robin Hood's fell short. Another legend claims that the distance between the pinnacles is the measure of Robin Hood's stride!

A path leads from the track towards Cratcliffe Rocks where there is a shallow hermit's cave, protected by two ancient yews, a low wall and iron railings. A seat, a shelf and a crucifix are carved in the back wall. The style of the cross and other evidence indicates that the carvings date from the 14th century and were probably the work of a hermit.

On Harthill Moor is Castle Ring and the remains of Nine Stone Circle. Another old trackway leads down to Bradford Dale and Youlgreave.

Although the Way does not pass through Youlgreave the village could provide a night's lodgings and is certainly worth a visit. All Saints Parish Church has an impressive 15th century tower and contains several interesting tombs and monuments. There is a most unusual font which has a tiny bowl on one side, presumably a holy water stoup. There is a large conduit in Youlgreave's main square with a capacity of 1500 gallons. Buckets were filled from a tap near the base. The 'new' Co-op was built in 1887. It is now a Youth Hostel but retains the original shop frontage complete with a carved beehive — the Co-op symbol.

The Way follows the path along lovely Bradford Dale. Beyond the second clapper bridge there is a series of simple dams with sluices which create still pools. Water fowl, trout and water weeds and flowers add to the interest of this tranquil dale.

A small packhorse bridge crosses the river and a steep, narrow miners' track winds up the hillside to the road and then past Lombersdale Hall, once the home of Thomas Bateman, a noted antiquarian whose collection of local relics is now in a Sheffield museum.

IN THE HERMIT'S CAVE NEAR ROBIN HOOD'S STRIDE

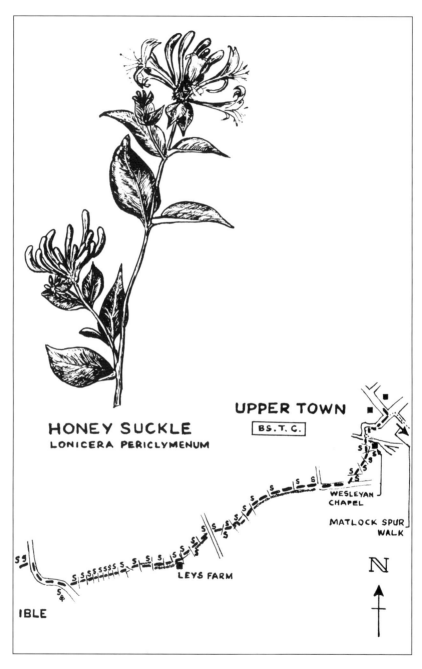

HONEY SUCKLE
LONICERA PERICLYMENUM

UPPER TOWN

BS.T.C.

WESLEYAN
CHAPEL

MATLOCK SPUR
WALK

LEYS FARM

IBLE

N

Ible — Upper Town

 South — North   **North — South**

After walking along road for 750 m take stile on L. Fp cuts off corner of field, making for stile concealed in hedge. →, parallel to line of wall on L.

→ through a series of narrow fields, finally following fence on R. After a stile just before corner of field fp follows wall on L. A further two stiles on fp again switches sides to follow wall on R.

Stay with field boundary on R to pass Leys Farm and bear slightly R to road. Cross road directly and bear slightly R to go through gap in wall. Then → through gap and stile, cutting off a tiny corner.

Skirt deep hole on L and resume original direction. Next fields are rough because of old mining activity, but route-finding is not difficult. Walk parallel to wall on L through first field, then by wall on R.

After a further three fields Upper Town is seen up ahead and Way passes by a small building and reaches a track. → down track for 165 m.

Just under ETL take stile on L and follow well-defined fp through a thicket. → towards Upper Town, finally winding down bank by houses.

At bottom, bridge ditch and →, passing Dale House on L and following Bankside as it winds steeply uphill. Having passed Yields Farm on R a further 80 m brings you to road intersection.

Way now takes road on L. Spur to Matlock follows road further up on R.

Walk down Bankside, with a good view across dale, to bottom. To R of Wesleyan church is a cottage. Way takes fp on R of cottage, winding up bankside. A clearly defined fp leads across fields and through a thicket.

→ to arrive through a stile beneath an ETL at a track. Turn R up track for 165 m. As track bends R, →, passing a small building on L. Follow wall on L for three fields.

In next field →, taking care not to stray L but walking parallel to wall on R. Go round deep hole on R to find stile in wall. Turn half-L after stile, following well-defined fp then → to road.

Cross directly over road and bear slightly L following wall on L. Pass Leys Farm on L and continue with wall on L. After passing a stile in this wall take stile ahead, then follow wall on R.

Ignore gateway on L and take stile ahead, still with wall on R. After next stile switch sides again so that fence is on L.

→ as fence bends to L to cross a series of narrow fields and head directly towards a large quarry. After a particularly narrow field → to a concealed stile 20 m below farm gate.

Cut off corner of field and reach road. Turn R along road for 750 m, passing interesting troughs on R.

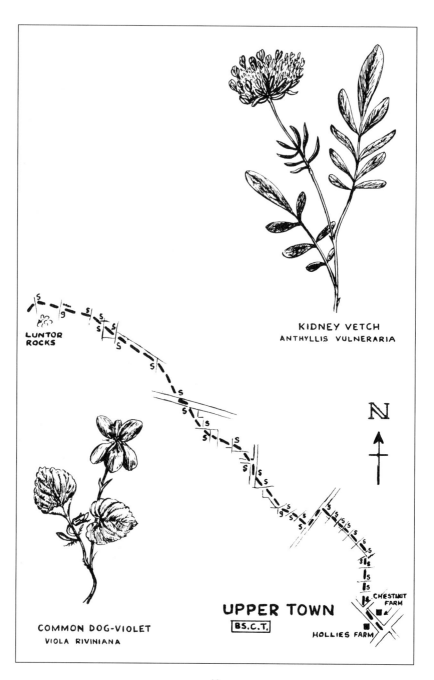

KIDNEY VETCH
ANTHYLLIS VULNERARIA

LUNTOR
ROCKS

N

COMMON DOG-VIOLET
VIOLA RIVINIANA

UPPER TOWN
BS.C.T.

CHESTNUT
FARM

HOLLIES FARM

40

Upper Town — Luntor Rocks

 South — North   North — South

From Upper Town you can take spur into Matlock (see page XX). To continue on Way turn L along road between Chestnut Farm and Hollies Farm (farm shop has minerals, ices, etc.). At road junction take stile with fingerpost to R ahead, turn half-R then → through four more stiles.

Here **bear L, ignoring fp leading straight ahead**, passing behind small ruined building. Continue with walls on L through seven stiles to Moorlands Lane (track, with fingerpost).

Turn sharp L and follow lane for 200 m, then R and proceed with wall on R. → for 500 m to Blakelow Lane. Turn R along lane then L **for a few m only**. Take stile on R and cross field diagonally.

Go through broken wall, bear slightly L then → to Bonsall Lane, a metalled road. Turn L along road for 70 m, then take stile on R into large field, turning half-R to aim for double electricity poles in centre of field.

→ past poles to stile, then bear slightly L to next stile and then slight R. → through old open-cast workings for four stiles, then bear slightly L with wall on R. Pass through a broken wall and a gateway to reach Luntor Rocks, with stand of larches, on L.

At this point Winster is seen ahead and a slight detour for a pub lunch may be considered. But to rest is not to conquer. To continue on Way, after next (rather elaborate) stile turn sharp L up bank then R to follow fence line at top.

When track degenerates into a fp and Luntor Rocks, with stand of larches, are seen ahead turn away from fence on R to go steeply down bank. Go over elaborate stile on R and turn R through a gateway.

Keep wall on L to a stile then bear slightly R and → through old open-cast workings for four stiles. Bear slightly L to next stile then slightly R towards pair of electricity poles.

→ past poles to road (Bonsall Lane). Turn L along road for 70 m then take stile on R, making half-turn R to go diagonally across field. → to intersection of two broad tracks.

Turn S along Blakelow Lane for 30 m then take stile on L, making half-turn to L from direction of lane (bearing 125° magnetic). → through five stiles to Moorlands Lane.

Here a fingerpost directs you to L along this sunken track for 200 m to a second fingerpost. Turn through a right angle to R then → through six stiles. Bear slightly R around small ruined building then → by a well-defined fp through five further stiles.

A fingerpost by last stile directs you along road (passing farm shop on R, with minerals, ices etc.) to road intersection in Upper Town.

Here you have choice between continuing in same direction, via Bonsall to Matlock, along spur (see page XX) or turning R down Bankside along Way.

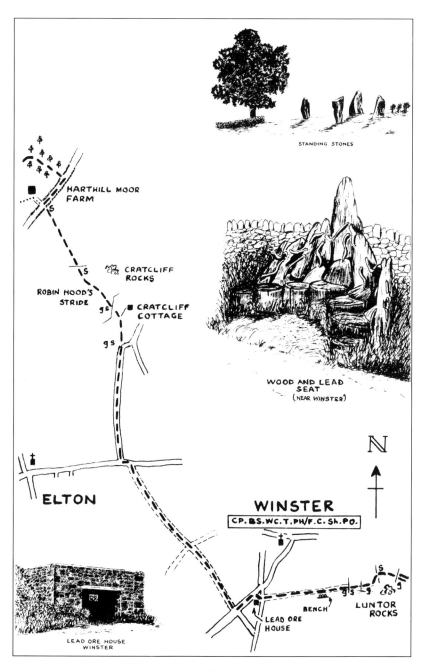

STANDING STONES

HARTHILL MOOR
FARM

S

CRATCLIFF
ROCKS

ROBIN HOOD'S
STRIDE

gs

CRATCLIFF
COTTAGE

gs

WOOD AND LEAD
SEAT
(NEAR WINSTER)

ELTON

N

WINSTER
CP. BS.WC.T.PH/F.C. Sh. PO.

S

LUNTOR
ROCKS

gs

BENCH

LEAD ORE
HOUSE

LEAD ORE HOUSE
WINSTER

Luntor Rocks — Harthill Moor

 South — North   **North — South**

Fp following fence on L widens into a clear track which broadens after a gateway. Follow broad track, with Winster down on R, for almost a km, to road (A524). Cross to lead ore house and → to road.

Turn L up road for 100 m then R along a broad track. Follow track for 1300 m to road (B5057). Turn L towards Elton for a few m (or carry on into village for refreshments) then R down Dudwood Lane for best part of a km.

Nearing bottom of lane you see ahead Cratcliff Wood and to its L twin rock columns of Robin Hood's Stride, which is on Way. When lane bends sharp R at bottom keep straight ahead into Cliff Lane, a private drive.

After 350 m drive bends to R towards Cratcliff Cottage and you bear L towards Robin Hood's Stride, along a grassy fp and an ancient paved way. At top of hill Stride is on L. On R lie Cratcliff Rocks and an ancient Hermit's Cave. Area is popular with weekend walkers and a pleasant place for a picnic.

Take stile by gateway on R, bear half-L, then →, heading directly towards Harthill Moor Farm and reaching road opposite farm drive.

A short cut via farm drive is now possible. To continue on Way turn R along road.

After 350 m up road, nearing brow of hill, drive to Harthill Moor Farm is reached on R. Ahead and to L lie twin rock columns of Robin Hood's Stride, which lies on Way. Take stile on L, opposite farm drive.

Head directly towards Stride. At top of hill Stride is on R; on L lie Cratcliff Rocks and an ancient Hermit's Cave. Area is popular with weekend walkers and a pleasant spot for a picnic. Bear slightly L and head downhill, following a well-defined fp, with wall on R.

Bear slightly R to follow track to gate. Take Dudwood Lane, directly ahead, and follow lane for about a km, emerging on Elton-Winster road. Turn L along road for a few m then R along a broad track.

Follow track for 1300 m. (Just under halfway along this stretch it is possible to make a detour to L if you fancy a pub lunch in Winster.) Track ends at a road along which you go to L for 100 m.

Cross grassy verge by lead ore house and main road (A524), taking broad track ahead. Follow track for nearly a km, with Winster lying below on L.

43

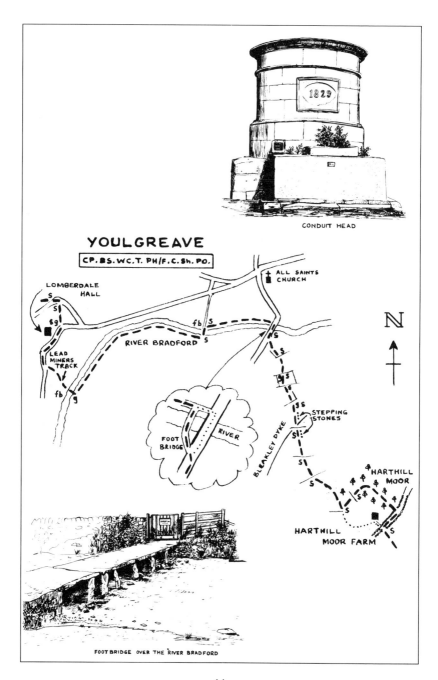

CONDUIT HEAD

YOULGREAVE

CP. BS. WC. T. PH/F. C. Sh. PO.

LOMBERDALE HALL

ALL SAINTS CHURCH

N

RIVER BRADFORD

LEAD MINERS TRACK

fb

FOOT BRIDGE   RIVER

BLEAKLEY DYKE

STEPPING STONES

HARTHILL MOOR

HARTHILL MOOR FARM

FOOTBRIDGE OVER THE RIVER BRADFORD

44

Harthill Moor — Youlgreave

 South — North   North — South ↓

Follow road for 350 m. Shortly after woodland begins on L take forest track on L and continue on this for 550 m, emerging at a stile into a field. →, first contouring then descending to another stile.

Turn sharp R to contour across hillside beneath ETL. On reaching brow of hill Youlgreave is seen ahead. Tower of All Saints Church in Youlgreave marks your direction for next km.

→ across Bleakley Dyke, via stepping stones in hillsides, to road (Hopping Lane). Turn R down road to bridge River Bradford. Turn L to take riverside path upstream. Youlgreave lies above on R and may be visited by any fp up bank side.

After 500 m along Bradford Dale switch banks, crossing by a beautiful old stone slab bridge. A further km brings you to a kissing gate after which you bridge river again, turn sharp R and ascend hillside, winding up by an old lead miners' track, a combe descending steeply on R.

At head of combe turn R along road for 400 m passing Lomberdale Hall on L. As road bends R take stile on L and ascend by a well-defined fp to main road (B5056).

On reaching B5056 turn L following road around bend and take stile on R to descend to another road, crossing to narrow pavement. Turn R along road for 400 m, passing Lomberdale Hall on R.

At an S-bend take an old lead-miners' track to L, winding down hillside with a steep combe to L, limestone crags to R. At bottom, bridge River Bradford and turn L to walk downstream.

After a km cross river by a beautiful old stone slab bridge. At this point you may continue up lane to Youlgreave. Way continues along dale, river now on R.

500 m further downstream brings you to road. Turn R to cross bridge and walk up road. After a short distance take stile on L. Your direction marker is lowest point in hillside ahead.

Follow fp by four stiles, taking stepping stones in hillside down to Bleakley Dyke and up other side. → until you bear L along a stretch of tractor track. When track reaches gate take stile by side of gate.

At this point a short cut is possible. By taking fp directly ahead you can reach road ahead, cutting out 700 m or so of walking (but also some quite pleasant woodland), emerging at end of Harthill Moor Farm drive.

To continue on Way instead of going forward turn sharp L, cross field and take stile to join a woodland track. Follow this for 550 m to road. Turn R up road.

OLD BARN

Youlgreave to Taddington

From the road west of Youlgreave wide tracks lead first to Calling Low and then to One Ash Grange, an extensive cluster of stone farm buildings of great interest. In 1147 monks from Roche Abbey in Yorkshire settled there and it is reputed to have been a place of confinement for unruly monks. Beside the path is a vaulted cave with cold slabs which was probably a larder or cold store. A two-seater privy is fronted by a large stone slab for a privacy screen (or perhaps draught excluder), and there is a range of magnificent pig sties. A barn has been adapted as a camping barn.

Monyash was once a busy market town and the northern lead mining centre. There were marble quarries in Ricklow Dale which were taken over in 1742 by Henry Watson, a Bakewell marble worker who established a marble works at Ashford in the Water. These closed in 1905 when Watson became bankrupt.

John Gratton, a famous Quaker, went to live in Monyash in 1668. There is a tiny Quaker Meeting House, now a Youth Centre, behind which is a small burial ground containing the graves of the Bowman family who lived at One Ash Grange in the 18th century, and were the last Quakers here.

The first St Leonard's Church was built in 1199 but it has been added to over the centuries and was rebuilt in 1887. A large chest, worm-eaten and held together with wrought iron bands, is believed to be 700 years old and once held the church plate and robes.

The present small village green in front of the Bull's Head pub has a fine market cross and the village war memorial. Like many villages Monyash declined with the lead mining industry but a small plaque states that Monyash received an E.C. award in 1985 for revitalisation and it is once again a thriving village.

There is a well-preserved pinfold on the road to Flagg. A board explains that this is a small enclosure where stray animals were impounded by the pinder and kept until reclaimed by their owner on payment of a fine.

From Flagg to Taddington the Way follows an ancient route along the now metalled Green Lane and rough track of Sough Lane which meets the A6 near the isolated Waterloo Inn. Near Five Wells Farm there are the remains of a chambered cairn which, at 1400 feet is claimed to be the highest ancient burial chamber in the land. The large capstones or covering stones have been removed but the remains of 12 people have been found. The cairn can be reached by a well-signed concessionary path from Five Wells Farm. As Sough Lane descends to the A6 there are fine views of the Way ahead. Miller's Dale is hidden from view but the tower of Tideswell's beautiful church, known as the Cathedral of the Peak, can be seen above the hills in the middle distance.

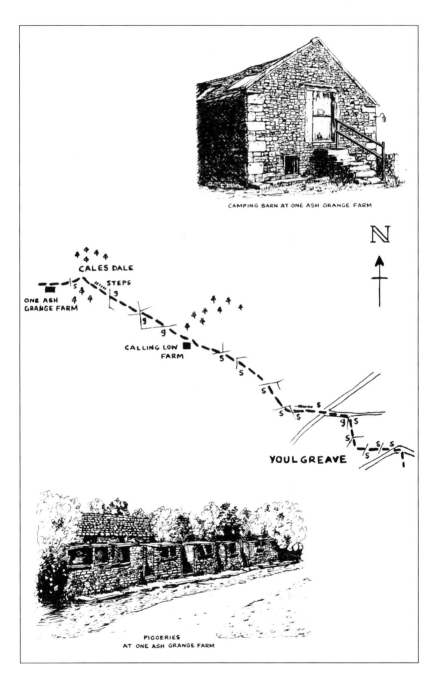

CAMPING BARN AT ONE ASH GRANGE FARM

N

CALES DALE
STEPS
ONE ASH
GRANGE FARM
CALLING LOW
FARM
YOULGREAVE

PIGGERIES
AT ONE ASH GRANGE FARM

Youlgreave — One Ash Grange Farm

 South — North   **North — South**

Turn L along B5056 for 60 m and take stile onto well-defined fp, climbing and gradually diverging from road. After 300 m Way becomes a broad track. Pass picnic area and → to road by Moor Lane CP.

Turn L along road to intersection then cross and → by well-used fp to Calling Low Farm. Signs and gates direct you around E side of farm, then by a gate downhill into Cales Dale. During descent to Cales Dale crags lining upper part of Lathkill Dale are seen on R. Ahead lies Monyash, next village on Way.

Descend to Cales Dale by steps and → across. A short steep pull up W side of dale brings you to a fingerpost directing you to L up a rocky defile.

Pass behind farm, using a stile between a large corrugated iron building on R and stone buildings on L. Follow clear directions around farm to emerge on farm drive by a camping barn.

At camping barn turn L to pass around farm, following clear directions. Just after large corrugated iron building on L take stile and → down rocky defile steeply into Cales Dale.

Turn R at fingerpost and cross dale to climb steps up opposite side. Walk through a series of gates to Calling Low Farm. As you ascend you can see crags lining upper parts of Lathkill Dale on L.

Clear signs and a succession of gates take you around the farm. Resume previous direction following a well-used fp over fairly level ground to a road intersection.

Take road straight ahead, signed Picnic Site. Just past Moor Lane CP on R take stile by gate and join broad track running alongside CP and picnic site.

After leaving track Way bears L quite steeply down to B5056 road. (*This may be followed to L into Youlgreave if you wish. Way leaves by a stile on R after 60 m and passes to S of village.*)

49

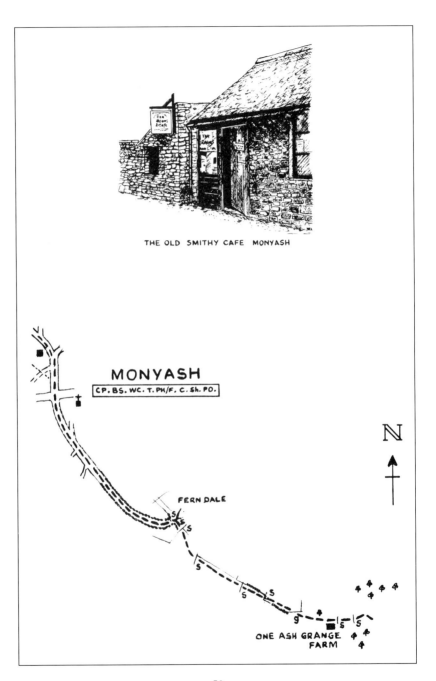

THE OLD SMITHY CAFE MONYASH

MONYASH

CP. BS. WC. T. PH/F. C. Sh. PO.

FERN DALE

ONE ASH GRANGE FARM

N

One Ash Grange Farm — Monyash

 South — North   **North — South**

Walk up farm drive, passing large barns on L. As track enters fields take metal gate on R and → with wall on L. At top of field **do not** go forward but take stile on L just before corner.

→, wall now on R. Descend into Fern Dale, a shallow depression running down to upper reaches of Lathkill Dale. Cross Fern Dale to take stile in corner of field then keep wall on L as you swing L to a walled track.

Follow walled track for a km, emerging on Rakes road, Monyash. Follow Rakes Road to crossroads with B5055 and village green, with old market cross, war memorial and Bull's Head pub.

Way goes along Chapel Street, directly ahead.

At crossroads and village green (with old market cross, war memorial and Bull's Head pub) → along Rakes Road. Follow road round to L. Go between farms to enter broad walled track. Follow track for a km.

Towards end, track narrows to a fp, at end of which is a stile. Climb stile and then keep wall on R for 50 m to another stile. Climb stile and cross Fern Dale, a shallow depression running into upper reaches of Lathkill Dale on L.

→, walking parallel to ETL on R, with wall on L uphill to stile. After stile →, wall now on R. Cales Dale lies ahead and in trees beyond may be seen Calling Low Farm.

Go through metal gate and → down drive of One Ash Grange Farm, past two large barns, to camping barn.

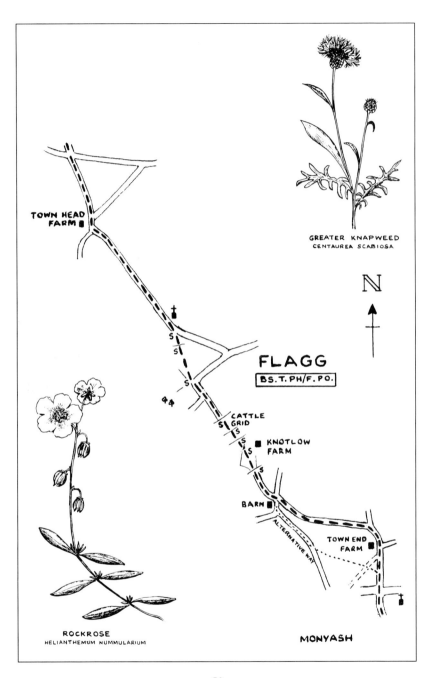

GREATER KNAPWEED
CENTAUREA SCABIOSA

N

TOWN HEAD
FARM ■

FLAGG
BS.T.PH/F.PO.

S
S

S

CATTLE
GRID
S
S
S
S
S

KNOTLOW
FARM

BARN ■

ALTERNATIVE WAY

TOWN END
FARM ■

ROCKROSE
HELIANTHEMUM NUMMULARIUM

MONYASH

Monyash — Flagg

 South — North   **North — South**

Walk along Chapel Street following signs to Flagg, Sheldon, and fork L towards Flagg. Pass Townend Grange Farm and pinfold on L. By next bend in road by Dale House (holiday cottages) turn L along Blackwell Lane, following Limestone Way sign.

Continue along lane for 750 m, when several tracks intersect by a barn. Pass a track on L (signed Hurdlow), then after barn bear slightly L along grassy track. Ahead and to R lies Knotlow Farm. Pass directly beneath ETL.

When track comes to a dead end take stiles, following fp signs and bearing slightly R to join farm drive. At this point Flagg may be seen ahead. → along drive and over cattle grid to join road.

→ along road for 250 m. As road bends sharp R take stile straight ahead and → across centre of field, then over two stiles to cut off corner of next field and join Main Road. Cross to pavement and turn L along road.

At next intersection keep R and follow road past Town End Farm on L.

Pass Town End Farm on R and →. 75 m after church on L find stile by metal gate on R of road. Take this stile and another to cut off small corner of field, then make for centre of next field and → to road.

Follow road as it bends L and →. After 150 m, at next R turn, → across cattle grid along farm drive (to Knotlow Farm). As wall on R leaves farm drive follow wall line. Take stile in corner ahead, passing farm on L.

Follow fp signs by stiles onto broad grassy walled track. After 250 m a barn is seen on R. Here several tracks meet and **care is needed**. Way bears very slightly L; to reach it, pass just one track on L.

750 m along track, by Dale House (holiday cottages), you reach road. Turn R along road into Monyash, walking along Chapel Street to crossroads.

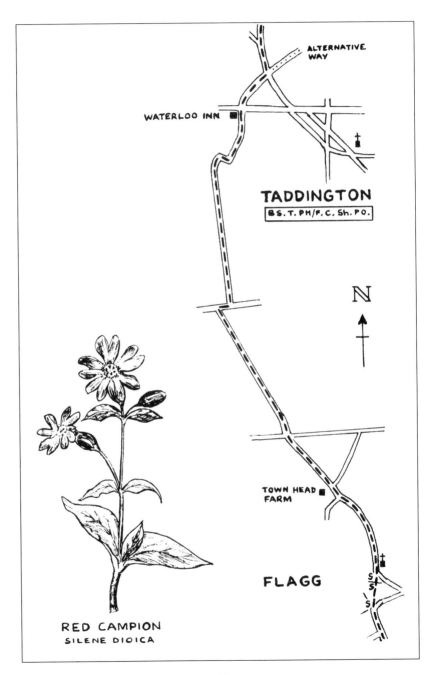

ALTERNATIVE WAY

WATERLOO INN ■

TADDINGTON

BS. T. PH/F.C. Sh. PO.

N

TOWN HEAD ■
FARM

FLAGG

RED CAMPION
SILENE DIOICA

Flagg — Taddington

 South — North   **North — South**

On reaching crossroads go straight across into Green Lane. Lane ends at a T-junction; turn R along Moor Lane and after 150 m turn L into Sough Lane, a deeply rutted and possibly very muddy track.

At highest point of Sough Lane you have a fine view of way ahead, dominated by Priestcliffe Low. Continue along Sough Lane as it winds down hillside and emerges on the A6 by Waterloo Inn.

Route of Way lies directly ahead, along Priestcliffe Road.

Cross A6 and take Sough Lane to L of Waterloo Inn. Follow lane as it winds uphill. Descending portion is deeply rutted and may be very muddy. After 1500 m on lane road is reached.

Turn R along road, then after 150 m L into Green Lane, a metalled road in poor condition. After 800 m at crossroads go straight across and → towards Flagg, passing Town End Farm on R.

. . . passed on the Way

Taddington to Castleton

The Limestone Way follows the Priestcliffe road to the first crossroads and then Long Lane to Miller's Dale. An alternative route goes through Priestcliffe, a scattered farming hamlet set on a steep hillside. From Lydgate Farm a well-marked footpath crosses several fields before skirting Miller's Dale Quarry, now a nature reserve, and drops steeply to cross the Monsal Trail and then the River Wye.

Near the impressive rail viaduct at Miller's Dale there is a Craft Centre and Workshop of great interest to wood turners and wood carvers.

The Way follows lanes to Monksdale House and Peter Dale but there is an alternative route through Monk's Dale, a hidden dale said to be linked with Tideswell by a secret tunnel and perhaps once used as a refuge in times of trouble. The path is very rugged and much of it follows stream beds and can be wet and treacherous. The dale is managed by English Nature who do not intend to improve access or the path as they wish to conserve the natural habitat. Woodland coppicing is carried out to encourage butterflies and plants, and sheep and cattle graze the steep valley pastures. Those with a special interest in the flora and fauna of an undeveloped limestone dale would find this route rewarding but slow.

At the end of lovely Peter Dale the valley widens out and there is an interesting ruin of farm buildings and, across the road, Curlew Lodge. Through Hay Dale the Way follows an old mining rail track. Behind a prominent chute there is an adit which is easily accessible. The path beyond passes through an attractive avenue of deciduous trees to a stony walled track. There is a sheepwash behind the northern wall. Note the modern farmhouse known as Limestone Way Farm.

Just beyond the point where the Way meets the A623 it crosses the route of the Roman road Batham Gate, which ran from Buxton north east to Navio, the Roman fort near Brough. Today many local tracks and footpaths follow this route and looking south-west from Mount Pleasant Farm the straight Roman road, which now leads to Smalldale, is clearly seen.

There are many abandoned shafts in the fields near the Way and from the hill crest beyond Copp Farm it can be seen that opencast working is still carried out. Mam Tor and Win Hill with the Kinder Plateau beyond are a beautiful sight for those walking from the south and after the quiet beauty of Cave Dale with its dramatic views of Peveril Castle it is startling to emerge suddenly into Castleton's busy market square.

Castleton is on the boundary between the 'White Peak', the limestone plateau and pastures in the south, and the darker gritstone, peat-covered moors of the 'Dark Peak'. There is much of interest here.

The castle was built by William Peveril, the son of William the Conqueror, soon after the Norman conquest and the keep dates from 1176. Local leadmining and hunting in the Peak Forest were controlled from here and one of the nine officials of the castle was the barmaster. St. Edmund's Church is also believed to have been built by William Peveril or his son and there is a beautiful Norman arch between the nave and the chancel. The unusual box pews date from the 17th century and some are carved with the names of 17th century parishioners.

A display case near the arch contains two rare Bibles, a Breeches Bible of 1609 and a Vinegar Bible of 1716. These are part of a library based on books bequeathed to the parish by the Reverend Frederick Farran who maintained a small lending library for parishioners. Some of the books are extremely rare and they are kept securely in the vestry though they can be seen through a glassed door to the left of the altar.

Around Castleton there are five caverns or mines where lead and spar were extracted. Blue John, a fluorspar containing a variety of blue purple and white bands in its crystal structure, is found only in this area and is still mined in Treak Cliff Hill and made into jewellery and ornaments which are sold in Castleton's gift shops. Odin Mine, where silver was found, is for experienced potholers only but Blue John Cavern, Treak Cliff Cavern, Speedwell Cavern and Peak Cavern are easily accessible and are open for conducted tours through the spectacular underground caves.

On May 29th each year Castleton commemorates the restoration of King Charles II with a Garland Procession when a 'king', with head and shoulders covered by a cone of flowers, rides through the village escorted by his 'queen' and the village band. A Curfew Bell is still rung from the church on winter evenings and at Christmas the main street is decorated with illuminated Christmas trees and the unique Castleton Carols are sung at the George Hotel.

Peveril Castle, Castleton.

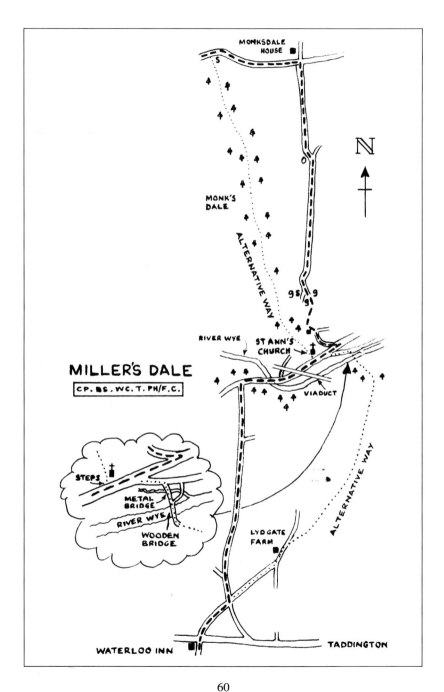

MONKSDALE
HOUSE

S

MONK'S
DALE

ALTERNATIVE WAY

N

9S 9

RIVER WYE

ST ANN'S
CHURCH

MILLER'S DALE

CP. BS. WC. T. PH/F.C.

VIADUCT

ALTERNATIVE WAY

STEPS

METAL
BRIDGE

RIVER WYE

WOODEN
BRIDGE

LYDGATE
FARM

WATERLOO INN

TADDINGTON

Taddington — Monksdale House

⬆ South — North   North — South ⬇

At Waterloo Inn cross A6 and follow Priestcliffe Road for 300 m to crossroads.

An alternative to Way into Miller's Dale now takes you straight ahead for 750 m to Lydgate Farm. Shortly after farm take stile on R and follow clearly defined stiled fp, descending steeply at last into Miller's Dale, bridge River Wye and turn L up a minor road, emerging on B6049 by St Ann's Church.

To follow Way, at crossroads turn L. After 100 m, when road bends L → down Long Lane. After 1.5 km join B6049 and bear R along road, using narrow verge on L to avoid traffic. At next intersection → (direction Tideswell), pass beneath impressive viaduct to St Ann's Church.

In fine weather another alternative may be used here. Take steps beside church and follow fp into Monk's Dale. Take clearly defined fp through dale for 2.5 km, emerging opposite stile to Peter Dale - see next section.

Way takes road on L just beyond church marked 'unsuitable for motors' for 70 m then turns L up rough track past Monksdale Farm. After 300 m track comes to a sticky end, unless weather is very dry.

→ to rutted grassy walled track. When track divides after 750 m take L fork. After a further 600 m you reach road by Monksdale House.

At Monksdale House take track on R for 1.4 km. After a gate → along metalled track, passing Monksdale Farm house on R. Track bends R and descends past barns on L to join minor road.

Turn sharp R down road to join B6049 in Miller's Dale, then R along road passing St Ann's Church on R.

An alternative route, avoiding a stretch of road, may now be used. Take minor road opposite church for a short distance, then fp on R, bridging stream and River Wye and climbing obliquely uphill. Skirt disused quarry on R and take stiled fp to Priestcliffe. Follow Priestcliffe Road to crossroads and → to A6.

Pass beneath impressive viaduct and after a further 600 m along road take roughly metalled track on L (Long Lane, part of proposed Pennine Bridleway).

After 1.5 km, when lane joins road, → for 130 m to crossroads. Turn R into Priestcliffe road, leading to A6, opposite Waterloo Inn.

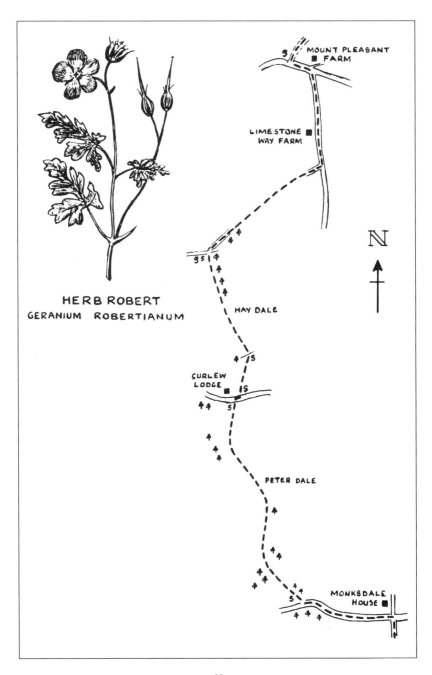

HERB ROBERT
GERANIUM ROBERTIANUM

MOUNT PLEASANT
FARM

LIMESTONE
WAY FARM

N

HAY DALE

CURLEW
LODGE

PETER DALE

MONKSDALE
HOUSE

Monksdale House — Mount Pleasant Farm

⬆ South — North   North — South ⬇

On emerging from Monksdale Lane at Monksdale House turn L along road for 600 m. At bottom of hill, shortly after a L bend take stile on R and cross pasture into Peter Dale.

Fp through dale is sometimes wide, sometimes narrow between limestone escarpments, but always clear. Finally, Curlew Lodge is seen ahead, across broad pasture. Take road opposite lodge and turn R.

After 40 m take stile on L into Hay Dale. A ruined chute on R is evidence of past mining activity. Mine adit lies above and behind chute. Pleasant path along avenue of oak trees follows line of old mine railway.

At N end of dale take stile and bear R onto a track going uphill for a km to join a road. Turn L along road for just over a km, passing Limestone Way Farm on L.

At crossroads you reach busy A623, with Mount Pleasant Farm ahead.

At brow of hill on A623, opposite Mount Pleasant Farm, turn R along road to Wheston for just over a km, passing Limestone Way Farm on R. A signpost on R now directs you down a stony farm track.

After a km on track bear L around a small limestone escarpment into Hay Dale, where fp follows line of old mine railway among a pleasant avenue of oak trees.

Adit to mine is passed on L, above and beyond remains of a loading chute. Dale bends R to join road near Curlew Lodge. (You may well hear curlews hereabouts.)

Turn R along road for 40 m, then L into Peter Dale, across a broad pasture. Fp for 1200 m through dale is sometimes wide, sometimes narrow between limestone escarpments, but always clear.

Finally, cross a pasture to a road.

At this point if you are prepared to rough it, in fine weather you could take an alternative path through Monk's Dale. Cross directly over road, take stile and →, following fp. Towards S end of dale fp bears L uphill then descends again to stream, finally ending by a flight of steps at St Ann's Church – see next section.

To continue on Way, turn L and follow road uphill for 600 m to Monksdale House.

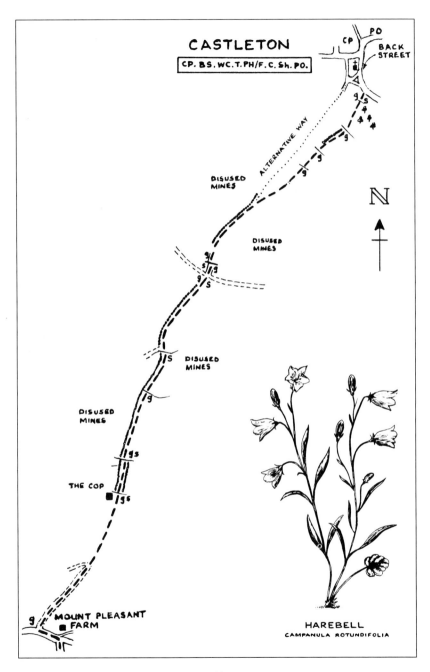

CASTLETON

CP. BS. WC. T. PH/F. C. Sh. PO.

PO

CP

BACK STREET

ALTERNATIVE WAY

DISUSED MINES

DISUSED MINES

N

DISUSED MINES

DISUSED MINES

THE COP

MOUNT PLEASANT FARM

HAREBELL
CAMPANULA ROTUNDIFOLIA

Mount Pleasant Farm — Castleton

↑ South — North   North — South

Turn L for a short distance down A623. A few m after a yellow grit bin take gateway on R onto roughly metalled walled track. White farmhouse ahead is Copp Farm, on Way.

Track becomes grassy and finally descends to road. Take stile or gate onto road. Peak Forest is now 1.5 km down road to L (information for those in risk of being benighted).

To continue on Way turn R up road. At Copp Farm follow signs to Castleton, skirting farm to L. Take stile on R and keep to fence on L, going through gates onto walled grassy track.

→, following track. On reaching brow → with wall on L. Directly ahead lies Lose Hill, with Mam Tor on its L and Kinder plateau beyond.

Shortly after a metal gate bear L, keeping wall on L and passing dew pond on R. After going downhill pick up wall on L again, following clear grassy fp.

Pass massive spoil heap of Hazard Mine on R and cross road →, bearing slightly R after small enclosure along broad track leading directly towards shapely cone of Win Hill.

When wall appears ahead bear R to pick up wall on L. Take gate, and follow well-used fp through Cave Dale into Castleton. Near bottom of dale ruins of Peveril Castle may be seen high on L.

From Market Place go uphill past War Memorial and follow signs to Way into Cave Dale. Walk up dale, ruins of Peveril Castle high up on R. After 700 m pass small wood on L. A spring rises here, so track often runs with water.

After a further 800 m limestone bluffs peter out and you follow wall on R, along broad well-defined track.

On reaching road a km later → following bridleway signed to Peak Forest, a grassy track. When track reaches a metal gate bear L, following wall on R uphill.

Pass dew pond on L and bear R with wall then →, finally joining walled grassy track. Bear L to skirt Copp Farm then follow road down past West View cottage on L.

When road bends R towards Peak Forest (1.5 km away) → by stile or gate to grassy track. After reaching brow Mount Pleasant Farm is seen ahead.

Track bends R then L to reach busy A623. Turn L to take road uphill.

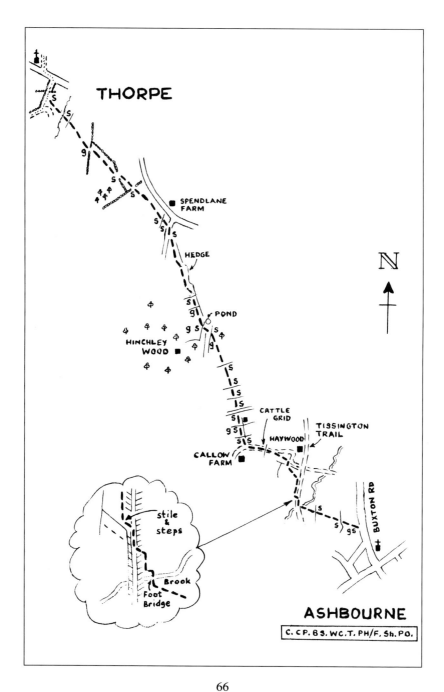

THORPE

SPENDLANE
FARM

HEDGE

POND

HINCHLEY
WOOD

CATTLE
GRID

TISSINGTON
TRAIL

HAYWOOD

CALLOW
FARM

BUXTON RD

N

stile
&
steps

Brook

Foot
Bridge

ASHBOURNE

C. CP. BS. WC.T. PH/F. Sh. PO.

The Ashbourne Spur

Thorpe — Ashbourne

At Thorpe Green, opposite St Leonard's Cottage, go downhill on grassy wasteland, fence on L. After 100 m turn R up track (Church Lane).

Half-way up Church Lane find stile on L. Descend directly to brook and → to highest point by manhole cover. → through gateway and → with wall on L towards Spendlane Farm, passing above a small wood.

→, farm on L, enjoying fine views across River Dove, to lane. Turn R down lane for 20 m then take stile on L. Continue with hedge on L. → when hedge bends to L. Pass corner of hedge and bear slightly L to stile in corner of field. Bear slightly R with hedge on L.

Just after a small pond on L take gate in fence on L, then **take gate ahead**. Bear slightly R, following well-defined fp. → across several fields to pass red-brick barn on L. Callow Farm may be seen ahead. → by two stiles to join farm drive. Turn L down drive for 170 m.

After cattle grid diverge to R of drive, following hedge line on R. On reaching drive again turn R through stiles into field. At this point, spire of Ashbourne Parish Church may be seen ahead. Cut off corner of field and bear R with fence on L.

Just before corner take stile on L and climb steps to Tissington Trail. Turn R down Trail for 25 m then L down steps and swing R, contouring parallel to Trail. Cross narrow wooden fb, turn L and follow well-defined fp uphill to reach A515 and end of spur. Turn R for Ashbourne.

Ashbourne — Thorpe

Take Buxton road (A515) out of Ashbourne. 50 m after crossroads and just before road-sign take stile on L. Descend hillside for 450 m, hedge on L. Farm seen to R ahead is next destination.

At bottom of field take stile in fence and cross fb. Contour for 75 m then swing L up bank by steps to Tissington Trail. **Turn R up Trail for 25 m**, then L down steps to stile. Turn R and walk up field, fence on R. Towards end of field bear L to cut off corner.

Bridge ditch, take stiles and walk uphill, hedge on L to join drive by cattle grid. → up drive. Just before L bend → through stile then bear R following fence on R. → more or less for 1 km, towards Thorpe Cloud.

Take a gate to cross directly over a ditch to a second gate and bear R, passing a small pond, to follow fence on R. After gate → to stile, then turn half-L to head against towards Thorpe Cloud.

On passing corner of hedge bear slightly R towards hedge line. Follow this hedge, aiming for Spendlane Farm. Go R up lane for 20 m then take stile on L signed 'public fp to Dovedale'. Pass on L of farm, enjoying fine view over River Dove.

At end of field →, cutting off corner of field. Head directly towards Thorpe Cloud, hedge and wall on R. →, finally crossing narrow brook. → to end of Spur at top of field. Turn R along Church Lane to Thorpe Green.

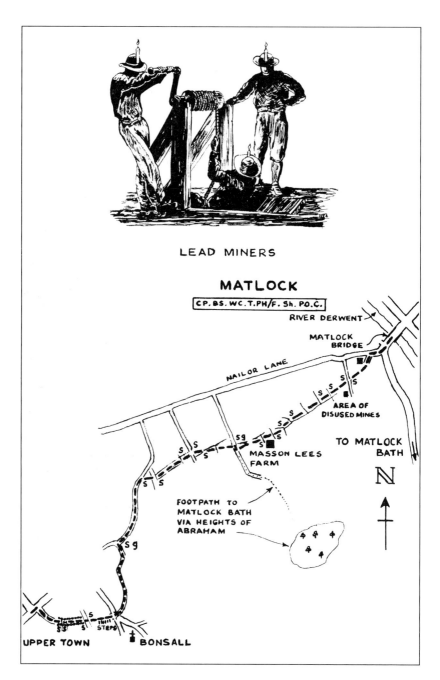

LEAD MINERS

MATLOCK

CP. BS. WC. T. PH/F. Sh. PO. C.

RIVER DERWENT

MATLOCK BRIDGE

NAILOR LANE

AREA OF DISUSED MINES

MASSON LEES FARM

TO MATLOCK BATH

N

FOOTPATH TO MATLOCK BATH VIA HEIGHTS OF ABRAHAM

STEPS

UPPER TOWN   BONSALL

The Matlock spur

Upper Town — Matlock

From Bankside, near post box and bus stop take road E between houses. → along walled fp, →, descending steeply by steps into Bonsall.

Pass cross, pub, → past war memorial on R and walk up walled concrete track. When track ends bear slightly L along (muddy) fp, contouring parallel to dale on L.

At T-junction of fps turn R uphill. At top of hill track bears R and shortly after this take stile on R, turning half-R across field, → along a broad grassy walled track. Ahead and to L lies Darley Dale. Later, as you mount stile into lane, you see Matlock ahead.

Cross lane and cut off corner of field. Follow fence on L and continue along well-defined fp to lane, noting Riber Castle ahead. Bear R along lane. After 25 m take stile on L.

Walk downhill with wall on L. Way is now clearly defined, passing Masson Lees farm on R. → along easily followed fp to emerge on Snitterton Road, Matlock. Turn R for town centre.

Matlock — Upper Town

From Matlock Bridge pass entrance to railway station (parking) and keep R to go up Snitterton Road. Spur starts 50 m up road on L. Go through farmyard and up steps.

→ uphill to cross a lane, following signposted direction to Bonsall. →, passing Masson Lees farm on L after a further km. Shortly after, on reaching lane, bear R along lane for 25 m then take gate on L.

Resume direction you were following before reaching lane, crossing field diagonally. Proceed with fence on R. Just before next lane take stile on R to cut off corner of field.

Cross lane and continue with wall on R, finally entering a wide walled grassy track. At end of this take stile to cross small field and join a lane. Follow lane for 300 m then take fp off to L (**could be missed by the unwary**).

On skyline across dale may be seen Upper Town. Fp leads to concrete track. → to road in Bonsall. → past War Memorial on L, cross and pub. → across road to fp between houses, up flights of steps then between walls on grooved flagstones.

200 m up this paved fp **do not** take stile on L but bear slightly R to walled fp in same direction. Final 100 m is along a road between houses, leading to a cross-roads, Bankside running across.

Way S runs down Bankside, to L. Way N goes along road almost directly opposite.

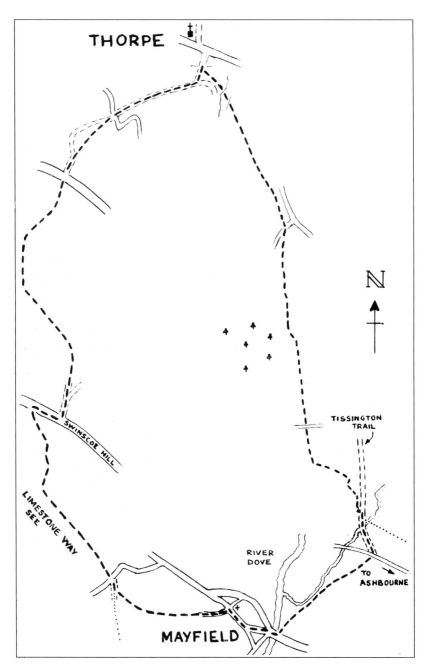

THORPE

N

TISSINGTON
TRAIL

SWINSCOE HILL

LIMESTONE WAY
SEE

RIVER
DOVE

TO
ASHBOURNE

MAYFIELD

Thorpe - Ashbourne Spur - Ashbourne - Mayfield - Thorpe

A pleasant day's walk through farmland, including a short riverside stretch and a visit to the attractive village of Mayfield

Follow Ashbourne Spur (page 67) as far as Tissington Trail. Turn R along Trail to southern end, a busy spot on a fine day in Summer, with a cafe and a bike hire depôt. If you want to see something of Ashbourne turn L along minor road; centre of town is only half a km away. To continue on walk, turn L up minor road for 30 m and take stile on R side of road.

Contour, then descend gradually, using stiles and finally following hedge on R. On reaching a fence, follow this as it descends gradually to stream. Sewage works lies ahead to L. Follow stream for 500 m.

When stream swings to R (to join River Dove) →. After a short distance a raised bank lies across the fp. Here diverge half-R to stile in corner of field. Take this and follow hedge on R, go through a stile by a gate, keeping fence line on R. A further stile takes you to rear of Royal Oak Hotel. Take Hotel drive onto main road.

Cross to pavement opposite and bridge river. Take minor road ahead ascending steeply to L of Queen's Arms Hotel. At T-junction at top of bank turn R. 100 m later pass Mayfield Methodist Church on R, then after a further 65 m arrive at a crossroads. Turn L along a street of pretty houses. When road dwindles to a farm track →, following public fp sign.

Go through a stile by a metal gate and continue along farm track between fence and wall, past a cattle grid. 50 m after cattle grid, as track bends L to Harlow Farm, leave it and →, hedge line on R, steeply uphill.

When you meet farm fence on L, follow this and then follow hedge line on L. Take stone steps up to stiles on each side of a ditch. → crossing another ditch and taking a stile in a hedge ahead. Bear slightly R, passing beneath an ETL by a post. A stile then takes you onto a track. You are now on the Limestone Way. Turn R along track, cross Stanton Lane and enter driveway to Lordspiece Farm.

From now on you can follow route directions (South – North) on pages 21, 23, to Thorpe.

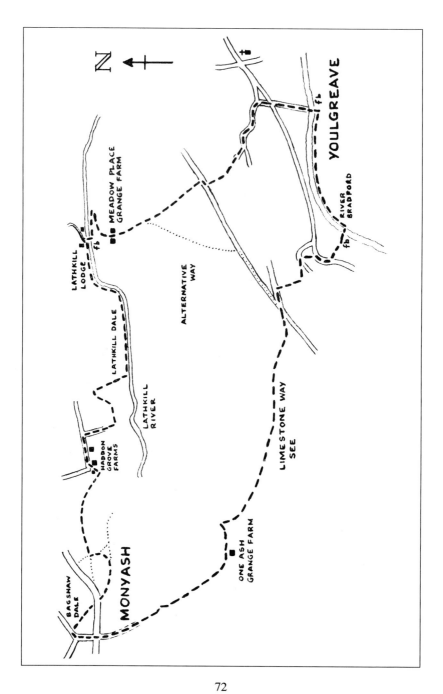

N

YOULGREAVE

fb

RIVER BRADFORD

MEADOW PLACE GRANGE FARM

fb

LATHKILL LODGE

LATHKILL DALE

LATHKILL RIVER

ALTERNATIVE WAY

LIMESTONE WAY SEE

HADDON GROVE FARMS

ONE ASH GRANGE FARM

BAGSHAW DALE

MONYASH

fb

Youlgreave - Monyash - Lathkill Dale - Youlgreave

This walk shows off nicely the wide variety in the dales of Derbyshire. It may be shortened from 16 to 13.5 km but this means missing an interesting section including the village of Youlgreave and an agreeable stretch of Bradford Dale. The walk includes some high stiles; they are well maintained but may not be to everyone's taste.

The walk starts at Moor Lane CP, GR 194645, which is reached by taking Moor Lane from Youlgreave for 1.6 km. The CP is on the L, just before a road intersection and lies on the Way.

Turn L out of CP and walk to road intersection. Follow Way (see pages 49, 51 South – North) to Monyash. In Monyash cross B5055 and continue along Way to end of Chapel Street. Leave Way, taking R fork (s.p. Sheldon) and after 30 m take stile on R s.p. Lathkill Dale. An easy decent through Bagshaw Dale takes you to B5055. Cross road and take stile into Lathkill Dale.

Follow broad grassy fp through two fields then **leave obvious fp**, bearing L uphill on a minor fp above Ricklow quarry, descending finally into Ricklow Dale. Turn L (N) along fp following wall on L. 100 m after a rocky outcrop on R a fp intersection is reached. Turn R here, following a fp sign then → by a series of stiles to a shallow dale. **In this section fp does not follow edges of fields**. Maintain direction making for a point in wall just L of clump of trees on hillside. Take stile here, follow wall on R past farm buildings and cross field diagonally.

Take stile and follow boundary on L past concrete ramp, then bear L down track (of Haddon Grove farm) to road. Turn R along road for 300 m then turn R into drive of Mill Farm (s.p. Lathkill Dale). A clear fp takes you to bottom of Lathkill Dale. Turn L for 2.2 km along much-used fp. At Lathkill Lodge turn R across footbridge and follow fp up through woods to Meadow Place Grange farm. Take indicated path through farm buildings to other side of farm.

Now you have a choice. *To take a short cut, bear R, following wall on R. By crossing three fields, a road and a further two fields you can reach Moor Lane. A 600 m walk R along lane takes you back to CP.* To continue main walk → following wall on L. On reaching road turn R for 35 m then L through two stiles. Follow direction set by two stiles and → by fp and track to Moor Lane. Turn L down lane and follow it to end in main street of Youlgreave. Turn R for a few m then L by telephone box down Holtwell Lane to Bradford Dale. Cross river by clapper bridge, turn R and continue upstream for a km. Continue along Way to CP. (See page 45, South – North.)

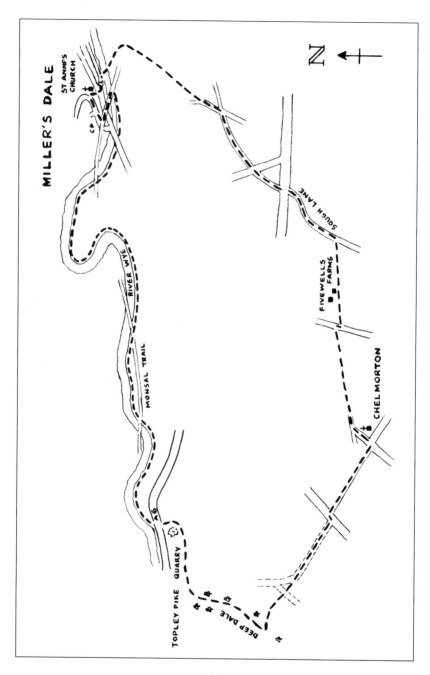

MILLER'S DALE

ST ANN'S CHURCH

RIVER WYE

MONSAL TRAIL

A6

TOPLEY PIKE QUARRY

DEEP DALE

CHEL MORTON

FIVEWELLS FARMS

SLOUGH LANE

N

Miller's Dale - Deep Dale - Chee Dale - Miller's Dale

Some rough going and some rather tame trudging are amply repaid by a day of splendid walking in dales country.

The walk starts at Miller's Dale Station CP, GR 137733, which lies a short distance up the road signposted Wormhill off the B6049 in Miller's Dale.

At entrance to CP turn L up road. At first bend take fp on R then → finally by ginnel and steps to B6049 by St Anne's Church. Follow Way (preferably using alternative route, see pages 61, 55, North – South) to Sough Lane. After 750 m lane levels out and in a further 400 m is crossed by a fp from Taddington to Chelmorton. Take stile on R and walk past Fivewells Farms on R to road. Turn R along road for a few m then L, resuming previous direction over ground disturbed by old mining activity. → towards spire of Chelmorton Church.

Take metalled road into Chelmorton. 80 m past Church Inn take fp on R, following Midshires Way (MW), to road. Turn L along road for a few m then R along track (MW). **Watch out for MW sign opposite second track leading off to L.** Take this track for 30 m then turn R over a stile and cut off corner of field to wall on R. → by stiles to Deep Dale, which is reached by a steep winding fp, passing a fine cave.

Turn R along rough fp in bottom of dale and follow dale, finally bearing L and skirting Topley Pikes quarry, to emerge on A6. Cross directly to CP and turn R to take track following River Wye downstream.

Just over a km later, at Blackwell Mill, you have the option of joining the Monsal Trail along the former Midland Railway line but Wye may be followed, with varying degrees of difficulty. After a further 3 km or so, just before a viaduct (used to practise abseiling) turn off L up steps to Monsal Trail. Follow signs to Miller's Dale; Monsal Trail passes through old station by your starting point.

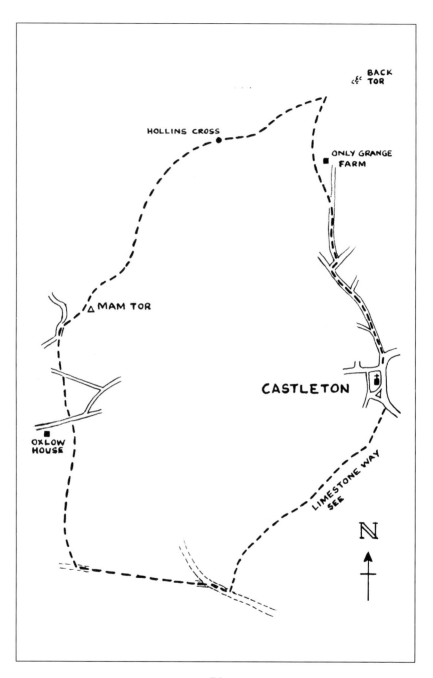

BACK
TOR

HOLLINS CROSS

ONLY GRANGE
FARM

MAM TOR

CASTLETON

OXLOW
HOUSE

LIMESTONE WAY
SEE

N

Castleton - Cave Dale - Mam Tor - Castleton

If you have a half-day to spare at the beginning or end of your long walk here is a shorter round with a taste of the Dark Peak.

From Market Place in Castleton walk up hill (Siggate), watching out for entrance to Cave Dale on R. Enter Cave Dale and follow Way for $2\frac{1}{2}$ km (see p 65, North – South) to mine road. Turn R along road for 200 m.

When main road swings R → through gate on to track and follow this for 750 m. At intersection of tracks, **just before gate** turn R to head N, with wall on L, old mine workings on R. Fp becomes more distinct.

Continue with wall on L. When Oxlow House is seen 500 m away, ahead on L, fp gradually diverges from wall (going directly towards Mam Tor) to reach B6061. Cross road and take stile by gate on to track, wall on L. → to A625.

Cross road and take stile for fp to Mam Tor, entering NT land. Broad grassy fp gives way to stone steps, ascending steeply to road. Carry on over stile to complete ascent of Mam Tor by further flight of steps and re-used paving flags.

Follow ridge path running N and E for 2 km, past Hollins Cross and over Barker Bank. At next col, as rocky scramble up to Back Tor appears ahead, drop down to R, take stile and follow fp obliquely down hillside, making for a small stand of trees.

→ through belt of trees by clearly defined fp passing Only Grange Farm away on L. Fp descends by a hollow way, wall on L, to an elaborate complex of fences, gate and stiles. Take stile and descend by roughly paved hollow way.

After 400 m tarmac road is reached. → along road. After a L bend, a further 400 m on, a track meets road. Carry along road (that is, turn R) towards cement factory with tall chimney, passing Hollow Ford Training and Conference Centre on L.

→, passing cemetery on L, to Castleton and end of walk.

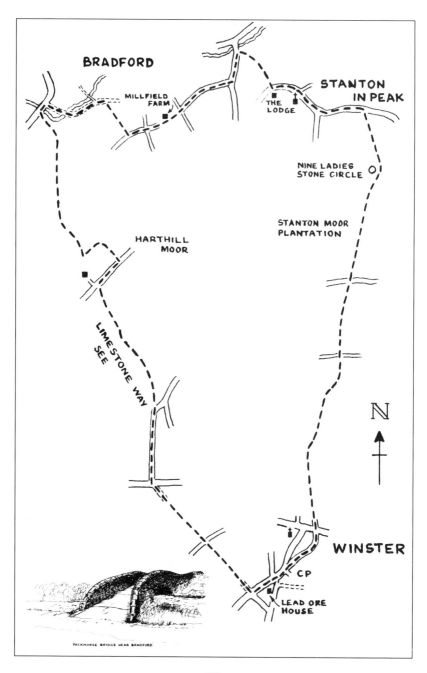

BRADFORD

MILLFIELD
FARM

STANTON
IN PEAK

THE
LODGE

NINE LADIES
STONE CIRCLE

HARTHILL
MOOR

STANTON MOOR
PLANTATION

LIMESTONE WAY
SEE

N

WINSTER

CP

LEAD ORE
HOUSE

PACKHORSE BRIDGE NEAR BRADFORD

Winster - Alport - Stanton Moor - Winster

13 km of easy going — a brisk half-day or a leisurely day; a little road work, nearly all on quiet minor roads; an interesting climax on high moorland.

Walk starts at parking space on rough ground above Winster, 100 m from Miner's Standard Inn, GR 238602. Walk uphill past triangle of grass on R then bear L along road for 40 m. Turn R along minor road sp Elton and Newhaven. Your are now on Way; watch out for Limestone Way sign on R. Follow Way (see pages 43, 45 South – North) as far as road bridge over River Bradford.

Cross bridge and take track on R, shortly following stream on L. Very soon after passing pretty bridge turn R off metalled way on steep grassy fp. Take stile at top and → with wall on L. →, passing by disturbed ground and a strange cairn on R, to farm track. Turn L along track. Cross over farm drive and → with wall on L, through wood.

→, passing Millfield Farm on L, to minor road junction. → along road ahead, passing caravan site on R. After 800 m of road turn L at T-junction along more important road for 250 m. 70 m before bridge take fp on R.

Walk up steps and take stile, then head E, hedge line on R. A further stile by a gateway leads you between rows of hawthorn trees. Where line of trees on L gives out take stile on R, heading towards Lodge of Stanton Hall. Turn L up minor road through Stanton in Peak.

After 800 m along road take L fork toward Stanton Lees. At brow of hill take stile on R to clearly defined track, then paved fp skirting woodland on R. →, then fork to pass Nine Ladies (stone circle, a popular picnic spot) on R. (L fork leads to a tower which is a good viewpoint.)

→ for 800 m across Stanton Moor Plantation. At crossing of tracks → down to road. Turn R up road for 40 m, then take stile on L to well-defined fp. Follow wall on L downhill. Pass Camping Barn on L and head S to pick up field boundary on R.

Follow boundary to far corner of field and take stile by gate. →, following hedge line on R. Cross track (Clough Lane) and → along track with hedge on L. At brow of hill Winster is seen ahead.

After next stile fp turns R and descends steeply through scrubby woodland. Continue to follow well-defined and sometimes paved fp across valley bottom and up to Winster by Woodhouse Lane. Turn L along main street then R before old Market Hall up minor road past Bowling Green Inn on L.

When road forks you can either bear L and stick to road or R, filtering L as you climb, through a network of ginnels. Either way takes you to common and starting point.

Glossary

Many of the terms commonly used in the lead mining industry are incorporated in farm, field and place names and the short glossary below may help to explain some of these:

Buddle – trough for washing lead ore;
Bole-hill – smelter site where the blast was provided by wind power;
Bucker – heavy, flat-headed hammer for crushing ore;
Gate – road, or literally gate;
Jagger – packhorse leader;
Jig – sieve (for riddling the ore);
Meer – length of a lead vein claimed, usually 29 feet;
Rake – trench where the ore was dug;
Sough – underground mine drain;
Stemple – steps in a mine shaft;
Stows – windlass or winding shaft; symbol of possession of a mine.

Bibliography

Mee, Arthur — The King's England. Staffordshire, Derbyshire
Pevsner, Nickolaus — The Buildings of England. Derbyshire
Dodd, A. E. and E. M. — Peakland Roads and Trackways
Spencer, Cyril — Walking the Derbyshire Portway. A Ramble through History (1993)
Defoe, Daniel — A Tour Through England and Wales
Willies, Lynn — Lead and Leadmining (Shire Album)
Parker, H. M. and Willies, L. — Peakland Lead Mines and Miners
Slack, Ron — Lands and Leadminers. A History of Brassington, Derbyshire
Rieuwerts, J. H — A History of the Laws and Customs of the Derbyshire Lead Mines
Merrill, John N. — Winster – A Souvenir Guide
Porteous, Crichton — The Well-Dressing Guide
Birmingham University Field Archaeology Unit — Rocester through the Ages (booklet)
Anderson, P. and Shimwell, D. — Wild Flowers and other Plants of the Peak District
Sterry, Paul — Regional Wildlife: Peak District (1995)

Scarthin Books also publish some sixty titles in the *Family Walks* series. For a current list please write to us at *Scarthin, Cromford, Derbyshire DE4 3QF*

01629, 823272